THE CARIBBEAN COURT OF JUSTICE

THE CARIBBEAN COURT OF JUSTICE

ENHANCING THE LAW OF INTERNATIONAL ORGANIZATIONS

Sheldon McDonald

The Caribbean Law
PUBLISHING COMPANY LTD

Kingston

Published in Jamaica 2005, by
The Caribbean Law Publishing Company
11 Cunningham Avenue
Box 686
Kingston 6

ISBN 976-8167-45-9

Originally published in a slightly different form in Fordham International Law
Journal 27, No. 3 (2004): 930-1016 by Fordham University School of Law.

Reprinted by permission of the author and publisher.

Cover and book design by Allison Brown

Printed in the United States of America

ABOUT THE AUTHOR

Sheldon McDonald is currently Project Coordinator of the Caribbean Court of Justice Preparatory Committee, CARICOM Secretariat. He was formerly Caribbean Community Lead Negotiator, Negotiating Group on Dispute Settlement, Free Trade of the Americas and is Deputy Permanent Representative of Jamaica to the International Seabed Authority. Prior to joining CARICOM he held a series of senior advisory posts and served as Special Adviser to the Attorney General of Jamaica and also to the Minister of Foreign Affairs and Foreign Trade of Jamaica. He has also served as a member of several Jamaican Delegations at International meetings and in negotiating a wide range of Bilateral treaties. Mr. McDonald's expertise in Law of the Sea and related issues is acknowledged nationally, regionally and internationally as is his expertise in International Dispute Resolution and International Trade Law (including the GATT, Competition Law, Investment, Intellectual Property and Services), the Law of International Institutions, International Human Rights Law, International Humanitarian Law and State and Organizational Immunities. He has also written widely in these areas.

THE CARIBBEAN COURT OF JUSTICE

ENHANCING THE LAW OF
INTERNATIONAL ORGANIZATIONS

INTRODUCTION

Whether one is concerned with the United Nations Convention on the Law of the Sea, the United Nations Conference on the Environment and Development, or the plethora of extant international legal regimes, developing countries, including the Caribbean, are accustomed to contributing in a significant way to the growth of international law and attempting to secure increasing respect for that law. Now, a grouping of ten small Island States, three mainland States, and one colonial dependency in the Caribbean has taken actions which will challenge the frontiers of international law.[1]

The establishment of the Caribbean Court of Justice ("CCJ" or "the Court") by the Member States of the Caribbean Community ("CARICOM") has already begun to contribute to the codification and progressive development of international law. At the present time, its contribution lies in the institutional architecture utilized in the design of the Court and the jurisdictional tasks assigned to it. In the future, it will be the manner in which the institution carries out those tasks assigned to it, and the manner in which its pivots – the treaty bodies – carry out their duties, that will

---

1. The Island State Members of the Community are Antigua and Barbuda, The Bahamas, Barbados, Dominica, Grenada, Haiti, Jamaica, Montserrat, St. Kitts and Nevis, Saint Lucia, St. Vincent and the Grenadines, and Trinidad & Tobago. Caribbean Community ("CARICOM") Secretariat, Caricom Member States, available at www.caricom.org/members.htm. The Continental Members are Belize, Guyana and Suriname. Id. Montserrat is a British Overseas Territory and requires Instruments of Entrustment from the United Kingdom to participate in the "new" Community. Id. Haiti and Suriname are purely civil law countries whereas Saint Lucia, and to a much lesser extent Grenada, Dominica, and Guyana have vestiges of civil law. Id. At this time, The Bahamas does not participate in the integration arrangements. Id. Given the new legal architecture of an integrated economy and institutional arrangements this is not legally sustainable. Id.

ensure its independence and sustainability. In both the procedural and substantive facets of the corpus of the law of international organizations and international economic law (and within both, regional integration law), the CCJ is on the threshold of taking them to new levels. The CCJ is an entity *sui generis*. On the one hand, the Court will serve as the judicial organ of CARICOM interpreting and applying the rights and obligations set out in the constituent instrument of the Community: The Revised Treaty of Chaguaramas Including The CARICOM Single Market and Economy (the Revised Treaty), ("CSME").[2] In the Court's Original Jurisdiction, it will be an international judicial tribunal basing its judgments, advisory opinions, orders, on rules of international law. This will give flesh to the plethora of new rights and concomitant obligations granted to, and imposed upon the Member States, Community Organs and Bodies, and, most importantly, to natural and legal persons. The Court has the important task of defining the contours and guaranteeing the observance of the law of the Revised Treaty, thus ensuring its supremacy, facilitating uniformity in the application of that law, and thereby contributing to legal and economic cohesion from the outset of the operation of the CSME.

On the other hand, the CCJ will also sit at the apex of the judiciary of those Member States that have chosen to adhere to its Appellate Jurisdiction, in substitution for the Judicial Committee of Her Majesty's Privy Council in England. The tribunal in this instance will be applying the Constitution, statutes, and the common law[3] of the country from which it hears matters as the court of final instance. The Commonwealth Caribbean Member States of the Community have decided on this step in order to complete the cycle of independence by patriating the highest judicial function. This unique legal craftsmanship is all the more surprising given the political ethos of the Member States of the Community, particularly as regards sovereignty. There is the recognition however, that for small States wishing to make their way in an often misanthropic world order, insistence on abstract, if not absolute, sovereignty often leads to the negation of that very sovereignty. In the words of the Basic Propositions put forward by the Expert Group of Heads of

---

2. Revised Treaty of Chaguaramas Establishing the Caribbean Community including the CARICOM Single Market and Economy, July 5, 2001, available at http://www.caricom.org/ infoserv.htm [hereinafter Revised Treaty].

3. The civil law Member States will not accede to the Court in its Appellate Jurisdiction for the time being.

Government in their report, *Regional Integration: Carrying the Process Forward* ("Regional Integration"):[4]

> The basic precept that CARICOM is a Community of Sovereign States acknowledges the ultimate sovereignty of the Member States of the Community. This does not, of course, preclude them in the exercise of that sovereignty, from pursuing collective action to deepen and perfect the integration process – as we have done, for example, in the case of the Caribbean Court of Justice.

The authors then go on to make the following fundamental observation:

> Indeed, we believe that the Community must explore diligently, other possibilities for the collective exercise of sovereignty by way of a creative approach to regional governance in cases where such an arrangement clearly advances the integration of our Community while maintaining its essential character. The collective exercise of national sovereignty, as in the case of the Caribbean Court of Justice, highlights our Community's special challenge of fashioning an approach to regional governance that is both functional and imaginative – one that could perhaps serve as a model for others to follow in the pursuit of innovative forms of integration.[5]

It is submitted that the latter statement is most appropriate for many developing countries wishing to carry out regional integration schemes, but wary of fundamentally compromising hard-won independence and sovereignty.

This Article will consider the following: Part I will discuss some general issues concerning dispute settlement internationally. Part II discusses dispute settlement systems in the Regional Economic Groupings, including the World Trade Organization ("WTO") (as evidenced in the infamous "Banana Dispute") and the future Free Trade Area of the Americas ("FTAA"), given that the Revised Treaty will be notified under Article XXIV of the General Agreement on Trade and Tariffs 1994 and will presumably be accepted as being consistent with the understanding thereunder. Part III will examine the Role of the CCJ as the judicial organ of CARICOM and the interplay between the original and appellate jurisdictions of the CCJ. Part IV will analyse the institutional and jurisdictional distinctiveness of the CCJ (including its referral procedure) and the features of the CCJ that make it *sui generis*. Part V addresses the role of precedent, *stare decisis*, and the rule of *Non liquet* in the regime and their implications for the interface of common law and civil law. Part V will also

---

4. Sir Shridath Ramphal et al., *Regional Integration: Carrying the Process Forward: Report on the Establishment of a CARICOM commission or other Executive Mechanism*, Draft 2.10.03 (Nov. 2003) [hereinafter *Regional Integration*].
5. Id.

include an analysis of the attitude towards precedent at the international level. Finally, Part VI will discuss *locus standi* for natural and legal persons and, to a lesser extent, the Advisory Opinion of the head of jurisdiction.

I. Dispute Settlement in International Law

The comprehensive work *Legal Problems of International Economic Relations* sets forth several general propositions of international law.[6] While one or more of these propositions may not represent current thinking on a particular issue, they are worth mentioning here:

- The theoretical bases for international law;

- The sources: customary and treaty law as well as the distinction and the interplay between these sources;

- The important aspects of treaty law, particularly the Vienna Convention on the Law of Treaties (1980);

- The relationship between international treaties and domestic law, in light of constitutional requirements for incorporation or the doctrine of the transformation of international legal obligations into the municipal sphere;

- The difficulty for common law students and practitioners to understand that a strict rule of *stare decisis* does not, and cannot operate at the international legal level, even while precedent has played and continues to play a critical role in the development of the international legal order;[7]

- Traditional international law has been deemed to provide rules that govern relationships between governments. Thus, the basic origin of international law suggests a very small role for individuals or private firms. Governments enter into a treaty, or invoke a dispute settlement process. When individuals or private firms have a grievance against a foreign government, typically they must go to their own government to provide diplomatic protection in the sense of carrying their case forward to an international forum. This can be quite confusing at

---

6. *Legal Problems of International Economic Relations* 244-46 (John Jackson et al. eds., 1995) [hereinafter *Legal Problems*].

7. As will be seen, this posit has largely been overtaken and in fact has been directly challenged in the regime. The discussion *infra* has been assisted by the contribution from my colleague Mr. Ronald Burch-Smith, Legal Consultant, Caribbean Court of Justice, Project Coordinating Unit.

times, and certain trends have begun to break down this different legal status for governments as compared to individuals or firms.[8]

The authors then go on to make the following observation:

> The role of the individual under international law, both as a legal entity obligated to obey international law norms and as a legal entity benefited by international law norms (such as human rights rules), has been evolving. This evolution has been particularly rapid since World War II and it is now generally accepted that individuals do have a certain international legal status.[9]

Ian Brownlie refers to this in the context of the diminution of the reserved domain of State jurisdiction.[10] This has been a feature of what has been termed the growth and development of the Charter Conception. This phenomenon has challenged the hitherto supreme rule of the Westphalian Conception. The latter obviously relates to the Treaty of Westphalia (1648), credited with being the birth-point of the modern Nation-State. On the other hand, the Charter Conception is linked to the United Nations Charter (the "Charter"), which has spawned the exponential growth and development of International Organizations (including those dedicated to regulating international economic interaction) that rival, if not supplant the State as the prime subject of international law.

The central purpose of the discussion is to examine the role that law as applied judicially, may or may not play, in the new Caribbean Community. Within the context of the Charter Conception therefore, it is appropriate to highlight certain of the bases of obligation under international law. This is important, because if obligations contracted do not fit one or more of these categories, then it may be difficult, if not impossible, for any dispute resolution process to operate effectively. Oscar Schacter identifies the following bases of obligations:

(i)   Consent of States

(ii)   Customary practice

(iii) A sense of "rightness" — the juridical conscience

(iv)   Natural law or natural reason

(v)   Social necessity

---

8. *Legal Problems, supra* note 6.
9. Id. at 245.
10. Ian Brownlie, *Principles of Public International Law* 291 (2003).

(vi)   The will of the international community (the "consensus" of the international community)

(vii)   Direct (or "stigmatic") intuition

(viii) Common purposes of the participants

(ix)   Effectiveness

(x)   Sanctions

(xi)   "Systemic" goals

(xii)   Shared expectations as to authority

(xiii) Rules of recognition.[11]

This list effectively incorporates legally binding precepts as well as norms grounded more in comity than in *de lege lata*. In any event, they represent the framework within the rule of *pacta sunt servanda* enshrined in the Vienna Convention on the Law of Treaties, which operates in inter-State interaction.

At another, wider jurisprudential level, the Charter sets out in Chapter I its purposes and principles. Article 1 is worth quoting in full given its direct bearing on our topic:

The Purposes of the United Nations are:

1. To maintain international peace and security, and to that end: to take effective collective measures for the prevention and removal of threats to the peace, and for the suppression of acts of aggression or other breaches of the peace, and to bring about by peaceful means, and in conformity with the principles of justice and international law, adjustment or settlement of international disputes or situations which might lead to a breach of the peace;

2. To develop friendly relations among nations based on respect for the principles of equal rights and self-determination of peoples, and to take other appropriate measures to strengthen universal peace.

3. To achieve international co-operation in solving international problems of an economic, social, cultural, or humanitarian character, and in promoting and encouraging respect for human rights and for fundamental freedoms for all without distinction as to race, sex, language, or religion; and

---

11. Oscar Schacter, Towards a Theory of International Obligation, from The Effectiveness of International Decisions (Papers and proceedings of a conference of the American Society of International Law)(1971), reprinted in *Legal Problems, supra* note 6, at 247.

4. To be a centre for harmonizing the actions of nations in the attainment of these common ends.[12]

Chapter VI, entitled "Pacific Settlement of Disputes," sets forth in Article 33 an explicit statement of the duty to resolve disputes peacefully: "The parties to any dispute, the continuance of which is likely to endanger the maintenance of international peace and security, shall, first of all, seek a solution by negotiation, enquiry, mediation, conciliation, arbitration, judicial settlement, resort to regional agencies or arrangements, or other peaceful means of their own choice."[13]

These and other principles and rules within the Charter have attained the status of peremptory norms of customary international law and are, concomitantly, binding *erga omnes*. That is they are binding without regard to volition or consent of the subjects of international law. Thus, even in a context outside of obligations under Caribbean Community Law, the States are under a duty to settle disputes among themselves in accordance with the foregoing. Finally, there are certain related principles referred to as "Corollary Principles." These are identified in the *Handbook on the Peaceful Settlement of Disputes between States*, the so-called *Blue Book*, as follows:

- Principle of non-use of force in international relations;

- Principle of non-intervention in the internal or external affairs of States;

- Principle of equal rights and self-determination of peoples;

- Principle of sovereign equality of States;

- Principles of international law concerning the sovereignty, independence and territorial integrity of States;

- Good faith in international relations;

- Principles of justice and international law.[14]

In particular contexts there is also the principle concerning the exhaustion of local remedies whenever applicable, and, finally, at the procedural level there is the principle of the free choice of means.

---

12. U.N. Charter art. 1, paras. 1-4.
13. Id. art. 33, para. 1.
14. *Handbook on Peaceful Settlement of Disputes Between States* at 4-7, U.N. Sales No. E.02.III.B.1 (1992).

II. *Dispute Settlement at the Horizontal Level*
of Regional Economic Groupings

Dispute settlement at the general level of the international legal order has to be distinguished from settlement within discrete regimes such as Regional Economic Groupings. This category of subjects of international law owes their currently elevated status to the success of the European Communities (now the European Union or "EU"). It is now widely accepted that regional trade and economic regimes facilitate the economic growth and development of the members and, additionally, can foster growth in world trade. However, these arrangements must have discrete dispute settlement rules, procedures, and institutional mechanisms. At the overarching level, the dispute settlement regime is concerned with the interpretation and application of the constituent instrument(s) and decisions or actions emanating therefrom. More narrowly, the system will concern itself with:

- complaints against Member States for non-compliance with the agreed rules, which may be brought by other member States, community institutions, or, as will be seen, by natural or legal persons with *locus standi,* where the constituent instruments accord such status;[15]

- complaints against the institutions of community, in actions brought by Member States, other institutions or natural or legal persons where they are given this right,[16] and

- the interface between domestic tribunals and Community tribunals including the duty of the former to refer matters to the regional tribunal or other institutions for the interpretation or determination of specific facets of Community law.[17]

It is necessary to place regional integration organizations within the wider ambit of entities that are subjects of international law and that, in consequence, dispose of certain rights and are subject to certain obligations, including international responsibility. In that regard, while the Congress of Vienna in the latter part of the nineteenth century witnessed the birth of international organizations,[18] it is nonetheless fair to say that the Conferences at Yalta and Bretton Woods, which led to the foundations of the United Nations System,

---

15. See *Manual on International Courts and Tribunals* 121-23 (Phillip Sands et al. eds., 1992).

16. See id.

17. See id.

18. One such organization is the International Postal Union. Prior to the United Nations there were organizations such as the League of Nations and its judicial body, the Permanent Court of International Justice ("PCIJ").

provided the greatest stimuli to the growth of those entities which today challenge the sovereign State for primacy in the international legal order.

In fact, one of the Bretton Woods institutions, the International Court of Justice ("ICJ"), would ensure that the organization could not be disregarded, ignored or treated with disrespect as a prime subject of the law. In the *Reparations for Injuries Case,*[19] the Court had to deal with the capacity of the United Nations to espouse international claims. The judgment stated among other things that:

> The subjects of law in any legal system are not necessarily identical in their nature or in the extent of their rights, and their nature depends upon the needs of the community. Throughout its history, the development of international law has been influenced by the requirements of international life, and the progressive increase in the collective activities of States has already given rise to instances of actions upon the international plane by certain entities which are not States This development culminated in the establishment in June 1945 of an international organization whose purposes and principles are specified in the Charter of the United Nations. But to achieve these ends the attribution of international personality is indispensable.[20]

The Court then went on to enumerate some of the faculties and describe the competence of the UN, including its enjoyment of certain privileges and immunities which create rights and duties between each of the Parties to the Charter and the UN.[21] From that perspective, "[i]t is difficult to see how such a convention could operate except upon the international plane and between parties possessing international personality."[22]

This prime example of the purposive, teleological interpretation of the constituent instrument of the UN led the ICJ to adumbrate the following view:

> the Organization was intended to exercise and enjoy, and is in fact exercising and enjoying, functions and rights which can only be explained on the basis of the possession of a large measure of international personality and the capacity to operate upon an international plane. . . . It must be acknowledged that its Members, by entrusting certain functions to it, with the attendant duties and responsibilities,

---

19.   Reparation for Injuries Suffered in the Service of the United Nations, Advisory Opinion, 1949 I.C.J. 174 (Apr. 11).

20.   Id. at 178-79.

21.   Id.

22.   Id. at 179-80.

have clothed it with the competence required to enable those functions to be effectively discharged.[23]

That naturally would lead to a conclusion that the UN is an international person. However, obeisance still had to be paid to State sensibilities:

> That is not the same thing as saying that it is a State, which it certainly is not, or that its legal personality and rights and duties are the same as those of a State. Still less is it the same thing as saying that it is a super-State, whatever that expression may mean. It does not even imply that all its rights and duties must be upon the international plane, any more than all the rights and duties of a State must be upon that plane. What it does mean is that it is a subject of international law capable of possessing international rights and duties, and that it has capacity to maintain its rights by bringing international claims.[24]

While the numerous caveats are clearly intended to, and still today do placate those with an essentially retrogressive view of sovereignty, the fact is that the UN is created to carry out certain tasks, disposes of certain rights and is susceptible to being impleaded under certain circumstances. This is as true for the UN, the EU, as well as the Caribbean Community. The way in which this ruling has become axiomatic in dealing between States and the UN may be seen as analogous to the fact that while precedent may not formally exist in international law except where specifically created by a treaty, there still remains the inestimable value of generally accepted or consensual practice – *jurisprudence constant* – often crystallized. Not even the most extreme opponent of international organizations would contest that the facets attributed to the UN have passed into customary international law. The practice of the United States is evidenced in *The Restatement of International Law*: Even when the United States withdrew from the United Nations Educational, Social and Cultural Organization ("UNESCO"), it accepted that at customary international law a duty exists to grant the organization certain privileges and immunities.

The Member States of CARICOM therefore must accept that by their actions they have created an entity, which, in Ian Brownlie's, words is "a permanent association of States, with lawful objects, equipped with organs."[25] Furthermore there exists "a distinction, in terms of legal powers and purposes, between the organization and its Member States."[26] Finally, just as critical to

---

23. Id.
24. Id.
25. Brownlie, *supra* note 10, at 649.
26. Id.

the legal personality of an international organization is "the existence of legal powers exercisable on the international plane and not solely within the national systems of one or more States."[27]

The criteria for legal personality in the CARICOM regime are fully met. The Revised Treaty of Chaguaramas sets out in Article 12 paragraph (3) the Functions and Powers of the Conference; the Supreme Organ in the following terms: "Save as otherwise provided in this Treaty, the Conference shall be the final authority for the conclusion of treaties on behalf of the Community and for entering into relationships between the Community and international organizations and States."[28] This function clearly requires international legal personality. In terms of the distinguishing of the powers of the members and those of the organization, this is evidenced in Article 80 on the Co-ordination of External Trade Policy. It stipulates, *inter alia*, that:

1.　Member States shall co-ordinate their trade policies with third States or groups of third States.

2.　The Community shall pursue the negotiation of external trade and economic agreements on a joint basis in accordance with principles and mechanisms established by the Conference.

This is to be contrasted with paragraph (3), dealing with the bilateral interactions of the Member States, which provides that:

3.　Bilateral agreements to be negotiated by Member States in pursuance of their strategic national interests shall:
    a.　be without prejudice to their obligations under this Treaty and;
    b.　prior to their conclusion, be subject to authentication by the CARICOM Secretariat that the agreement does not prejudice or place at a disadvantage the position of other CARICOM States vis-a vis the Treaty.

The requirement of the fourth paragraph is even more stringent:

4.　Where trade agreements involving tariff concessions are being negotiated, the prior approval of the Council for Trade and Economic Development shall be required.[29]

27.　Id.
28.　Revised Treaty, *supra* note 3, art. 12, para. 3.
29.　Id. art. 80.

A. Dispute Settlement in International Economic Law: Comments on the World Trade Organization ("WTO") and the Emerging FTAA

All commentators are agreed that the results of the Uruguay Round of multilateral trade negotiations, codified in the Marrakesh Agreements Establishing the WTO have brought a significant measure of coherence to the legal and institutional framework of international economic law. The Dispute Settlement System ("DSS") within the regime has been improved beyond recognition:

> [T]he Uruguay Round has entered into history as a unique achievement, indeed a transitio ad alterum genus, in comparison to all the preceding "rounds." This applies also to dispute settlement, which moved from its hitherto marginal position to become, as is said in Article 3.2 of the Understanding, a "central element" in the new trading system."[30]

The former President of the European Court of Justice, Pierre Pescatore, considers the following to be the "strong points" of the new multilateral regime:

> (1) the system has been in many respects brought up to a higher level of legal effectiveness; (2) the, so far, essentially normative provisions of the various agreements have been embedded into an institutional structure; (3) the unity of the system of dispute settlement, which had been breaking apart after the Tokyo Round, has been restored; (4) a bridge has been opened from sectorial isolationism of "GATT law" to general international law; (5) the system of sanctions has been recognized in a multilateral framework; (6) finally, we may note that all those procedural devices which had proved to be essential for the effective functioning of the old GATT mechanism have been taken over integrally into the new system.[31]

This "impressive record" has "radically cured" the prevailing uncertainty by virtue of the fact that:

> the WTO Agreements have been negotiated in the form of regular international treaties, entered into in conformity with the constitutional provisions of the members. By this, the provisions relating to dispute settlement benefited from *a double upgrade*: not only have they been embodied in a formal Understanding, but the same Understanding, in virtue of Article II:2 of the WTO Agreement, has received the same legal authority as the constitutive instrument itself, of which it makes an integral part.[32]

---

30. Pierre Pescatore, 'The New WTO Dispute Settlement Mechanism', in *Regionalism and Multilateralism After the Uruguay Round* 661 (Paul Demaret et al. eds., 1997).
31. Id. at 662.
32. Id. (emphasis in original).

The result of the termination of this "legal vagrancy"[33] has been to create in the WTO a DSS with a "three-tier logic comprising: (a) nullification and impairment of trade benefits; (b) frustration of the organization's objectives; (c) disregard of obligations flowing from the organization's constitutive instrument and from the rules governing dispute settlement."[34] While the old system did relate to general international law, all agreed that the relationship has been made "more explicit, not only through the mode of setting up the organization, but also by "the express recognition, in Article 3:2 of the Understanding, that dispute settlement serves to clarify the existing provisions of the various agreements 'in accordance with customary rules of interpretation of public international law.'"[35]

It is a very short step to conclude that this refers "essentially" to the rules of interpretation as codified in the Vienna Convention on the Law of Treaties. The instrument has formed parts of ruling of panels, and as discussed above, Pescatore identifies the following provisions of the Convention relevant to regulating the law in this area:

- international treaties are binding and must be implemented and interpreted in good faith (Articles 26 and 31);
- internal legislation is no excuse for failure to implement a treaty obligation (Article 27);
- treaty provisions are, in principle, non-retroactive (Article 28);
- treaty obligations coincide normally with the sphere of territorial jurisdiction of States (Article 29);
- treaties must be interpreted in good faith, in accordance with the ordinary meaning of their terms, in context and in light of their objects and purpose (Articles 31-32);
- linguistic difficulties, in case of multilingual treaties, are to [sic] resolved also by the object-and-purpose test (Article 32).[36]

While being hortatory, two paragraphs of the Convention are deemed to be of importance when dealing with this facet of the international legal order. These are paragraphs 3, relating to the principle of good faith and the "universally" recognized rule of *pacta sunt servanda*, and paragraph 8, which stipulates that: "the rules of customary international law will continue

33. Id.
34. Id. at 666.
35. Id.
36. Id. at 667.

to govern questions not regulated by the provisions of the present Convention."[37]

B. Elements of the General and Institutional Provisions: Including the Dispute Settlement Chapter of the Second Draft of the FTAA Agreement (the "Second Draft")[38]

Having cursorily examined the multilateral dimension of the issue, it is now useful to consider some of the FTAA provisions which either directly or indirectly impact upon the Revised Treaty of Chaguaramas, as will be notified under Article XXIV of the GATT 1994 and the Understanding thereunder.

The FTAA will bring together thirty-four of some of the territorially and economically largest and smallest countries in the world. It will group resource-endowed and resource-challenged societies. In all of this, one has to bear in mind that the neo-theological dictates of globalization and liberalization are often quite unmindful of size or capacities in its seemingly inexorable "thrust" forward (mass protests notwithstanding).

At the same time, this attempt at creating a new regional economic integration regime, will bring together States which are themselves part of [sub]-regional integration movements – Mercosul, CARICOM, the Andean Community and the Central American Common Market. A significant legal and jurisprudential challenge, therefore, exists to secure the competence of these entities even while creating a coherent hemispheric regime. It would be appropriate, as well, to be mindful of the political and economic strategy propelling this initiative.

A major issue in the Negotiating Group on Dispute Settlement in the early stages of the process was the issue of the legal and juridical relationship between the FTAA and existing regional economic integration movements. The issue was ultimately settled by the Trade Ministers, along with other institutional questions that were deemed to be "cross-cutting issues." The majority of countries would not be persuaded that the new entity would be legally superior to, and form the juridical apex of, their international economic interaction. The fact that the more appropriate view prevailed is evidenced in the Preamble.[39]

---

37. Id.
38. See FTAA – Free Trade Area of the Americas, Second Draft Agreement, Nov. 1, 2002, FTAA.TNC/w/133/Rev.2, available at http://www.ftaa-alca.org/ftaadraft02/draft_e.asp (not yet entered into force) [hereinafter Second Draft].
39. Id. at Preamble to the FTAA Agreement.

The text is replete with square brackets, but for present purposes, only those contained within the provisions to be cited will be reproduced. The legal and juridical relationship issue is dealt with in two paragraphs. The Preamble speaks of the prospective parties "[c]onsidering their respective rights and obligations under the World Trade Organization agreements and other multilateral, regional and subregional instruments of integration and co-operation."[40] In the second reference, the parties speak of "removing to the extent possible, consistent with Article XXIV of the GATT 1994, other restrictive regulations of commerce."[41]

The latter paragraph is of obvious importance to the existing regional economic groupings. Having notified under the cited provision, and having "passed muster" at the Working Group level,[42] they are allowed certain external flexibilities as long as, on the whole, the measures adopted do not appear to be more trade restrictive than those existing prior to the grouping being formed.

The Preamble, following the recent practice described above by Pescatore, but achieved over the objections of certain major players, also makes clear that the participating countries are "[c]onvinced of the importance of creating effective procedures for the *interpretation and application* of this agreement, for its joint administration and for the resolution of disputes among the Parties."[43]

Articles 3 and 4 of the General Articles of the Second Draft, dealing with, respectively, Principles and the Application and Scope of the agreement, track the relationship issue in the following terms:

a. consistency of the rights and obligations emanating from this Agreement with the rules and disciplines of the World Trade Organization;[44] and

b. the co-existence of this Agreement with bilateral and sub-regional agreements, to the extent that the rights and obligations deriving from these agreements are greater in scope than those hereunder.[45]

In terms of the Scope of Application, paragraph 3 of Article 4 declares that the new agreement shall "co-exist with bilateral and sub-regional agreements. . . ."[46] Furthermore, the new agreement "does not adversely affect the rights and obligations that one or more Parties may have under such agreements, to the

---

40. Id.
41. Id.
42. See id. at Draft Chapter on Dispute Settlement, art. 10, para. 55.
43. Id. at Preamble to the FTAA Agreement (emphasis added).
44. Id. at General Articles of the FTAA Agreement, art. 3c.
45. Id. art. 3d.
46. Id. art. 4, para. 4.3.

extent that such rights and obligations imply a greater degree of integration than provided for hereunder."[47]

By virtue of the next paragraph, the negotiating partners "confirm the rights and obligations in force among them under the WTO Agreement."[48] Still, there is an important caveat: "In the event of conflict between the provisions of the WTO Agreement and the provisions of this Agreement, the provisions of this Agreement shall prevail to the extent of the conflict."[49]

This rule is going to provide the basis for major litigation, as the partners in the North American Free Trade Area ("NAFTA") seek to write higher levels of, and/or new, rules and disciplines in relation to such areas as Investment Policy,[50] Competition Policy,[51] Intellectual Property Rights,[52] Government Procurement,[53] and, in terms of institutional and dispute settlement matters, the participation of non-State entities in the procedures of the organization.[54]

The Draft Text on General and Institutional issues also contains a notification requirement where members enter into international agreement in cases where the latter "refer to matters covered in" the FTAA Agreement.[55] Finally, there is an interesting Review and Appeal procedure, which requires the establishment or maintenance of judicial, quasi-judicial, or administrative entities to review and correct "measures of general application" which presumably impact on the agreement.[56] The second sentence of this provision has a link with the case law of the ECJ in terms of the Preliminary Ruling Procedure discussed later in this Article.[57] The provision states that the tribunals entrusted with the review or appeal "[shall be impartial and independent of the office or authority entrusted with [administrative enforcement [of the law]] [to apply measures of general application respecting

---

47 Id.

48. Id. art. 4, para. 4.4.

49. Id.

50. See generally id. at Draft Chapter on Investment.

51. See generally id. at Draft Chapter on Competition Policy.

52. See generally id. at Draft Intellectual Property Rights Chapter.

53. See generally id. at Draft Chapter on Government Procurement.

54. See generally id. at Draft Chapter on Dispute Settlement.

55. Id. at Draft Text on General and Institutional Issues, art. 8.3.

56. Id. art. 11.1.

57. See *infra* notes 164-165 and accompanying text; see generally *Dorsch Consult Ingenieurgesellschaft v. Bundesbaugesellschaft Berlin*, Case C-54/96 [1997] E.C.R. I-4961.

any matter covered by this Agreement,] and shall not have any substantial interest in the outcome of the matter.]"[58]

Of even greater significance, at least judicially, is that the CCJ, in interpreting and applying the constituent instrument of the Caribbean Community, may be invited to, and may even on its own volition, take judicial notice of the newer regime. However, it would be entirely within its right to regard the latter as *res inter alios actos*, or to opt to go in the direction of the European Court in the *ERTA* and subsequent line of cases.[59] A Caribbean Court faithful to its tasks will ensure that the Member States, in carrying out the obligations of the FTAA, do not infringe the rules in Article 80 of the Revised Treaty. Article 45 of the Dispute Settlement Chapter of the FTAA provides a measure of flexibility. The provision contains rules dealing with the interpretation of the latter agreement in judicial or administrative proceedings of a party.[60] Given the fundamental posit of this Article, consistent with the Revised Treaty and the Agreement Establishing the CCJ, the context requires that the proceeding addressed in Article 45 of the Dispute Settlement Chapter of the FTAA and its reference to a municipal tribunal must be read to mean the regional court.

Article 43 of the Dispute Settlement Chapter of the FTAA gives the party in whose territory the judicial or administrative proceedings are being held the duty to notify the FTAA Secretariat, if it "considers . . . [that the issue of interpretation or application] . . . merits its intervention, or if a judicial …body solicits the views of one of the Parties …[to the FTAA]."[61] While the procedure adopted is that the Executive Body for Dispute Settlement will strive to find a non-binding position to put forward, the more important point is that the judicial body has the authority to regard the position as a factual statement, not a statement of the law. The Member States of the Community, the Office of General Counsel, and the Legal Affairs Committee will therefore have to be vigilant to ensure that no matter comes before the regional judicial body in which a FTAA issue is being raised, directly or indirectly, and to ensure that they do not intervene, if only not to cause embarrassment to particular Member States. Similar vigilance will be needed in situations where Member States of the Community purport to implement FTAA-consistent, but WTO-inconsistent, measures and where these have a negative, or at least a detrimental,

---

58. Second Draft, *supra* note 38, at Draft Text on General and Institutional Issues, General Articles of the FTAA Agreement, art. 11.1.

59. See *infra* note 235 and accompanying text.

60. See Second Draft, *supra* note 38, at Draft Chapter on Dispute Settlement, art. 45.

61. Id. art. 43, para. 222.

impact on the Single Market and Economy sufficient enough to cause proceedings to be instituted in the CCJ.

Apart from the foregoing, there are some other issues within the dispute settlement regime of the proposed FTAA that the negotiators for the Caribbean Community and other regional groupings may wish to study carefully. They include:

1. The Article 4 assertion of the Dispute Settlement Chapter that the intent of the dispute resolution system is to ensure the application of agreed principles and to maintain "a balance between rights and obligations of the Parties";[62] and the assertion that the DSS is there to "preserve the rights and obligations of the Parties...and to clarify the existing provisions...in accordance with customary rules of interpretation of public international law."[63] Will the major players in the new regime agree that the Right to Development has passed from *de lege ferenda* to *lex lata* and into customary international law? Even now the norm of State sovereignty over natural resources is being challenged as a rule of customary law.

2. Then, there is the issue of choice of forum, set out in Article 6 of the Dispute Settlement Chapter. The Members of CARICOM must ensure that the adopted text incorporates the right of its Members *inter se* to settle disputes among themselves on matters which impact upon the Revised Treaty, as the FTAA is bound to do within their own forum.

3. In terms of Multiple Complaints, the Chapter on Dispute Settlement, as presently structured, limits the right of Member States to initiate judicial proceedings at any time, if they choose not to be enjoined as a Complaining Party under the FTAA procedures. Again, the CARICOM negotiators – and those from whom they receive their instructions – need to re-examine this provision closely.

It may be apposite to remind all concerned that the legal and juridical distance between the matters regulated under the WTO, the FTAA, and the Revised Treaty are merely words away.

C. *The Jurisprudential Bases for the Revised Dispute Settlement Regime*

A fundamental question that arises in constructing and evaluating dispute settlement systems at the international level is whether the systems should be primarily designed

---

62. Id. art. 4, para. 24.
63. Id. art. 4, para. 2.

to adjudicate disputes or to mediate them. If mediation is the goal, then a dispute settlement system must emphasize methods designed to encourage the contending parties to negotiate a solution to their dispute. If adjudication is the goal, then a system must be able to apply the relevant rules consistently and ensure that the decisions produced by the system are implemented.[64]

The commentary and analysis in the Reports of the Inter-Governmental Tasks Force, which elaborated the Revised Treaty, would show that the Caribbean regional integration movement does not believe that the solution must be either mediation or adjudication. The experience of the past thirty years has shown, through the dismal failure of the former to weld together a tightly-knit process, that optimal utilization of adjudication can only assist the process. Therefore, a key element of the policy can be couched in the following terms:

> In the interest of the development, economic and social progress of the Member States of CARICOM and their nationals, this tier of dispute settlement has to be put in place. The Gentleman's agreement mode has been tried and tested and found severely wanting. The system now desperately needs an injection of the rule-based approach to which CARICOM is subjected, in any event, at the multilateral level and to which it is to be subjected, imminently, at the hemispheric level.[65]

John Jackson posits a list of "policies that underlie the way that institutions and procedures have been shaped within the United States"[66] in terms of the application of dispute settlement involving international economic and trade interactions. Although written as an *apologia* for American unilateralism in the global trading system, the procedures, standing on their own, represent the kind of ideals to which the entire Single Market and Economy aspires, and within that regime, the dispute settlement system. The policies are as follows:

(1) The procedure should maximize the opportunity of government officials to receive all relevant information, arguments, and perspectives. Thus, a procedure that allows all interested parties to present evidence and arguments would enhance the realization of this goal.

---

64. *Legal Problems,supra* note 6, at 327-28.
65. Sheldon McDonald, 'Signposts to the Development of Judicial Institutions in the Caribbean Community — The Advisory Opinion Jurisdiction and the Referral Procedure of the Agreement Establishing the CCJ' (2000) (unpublished article) (on file with author).
66. John Jackson, 'Perspectives on the Jurisprudence of International Trade: Costs and Benefits of Legal Procedures in the United States', 82 Mich. L. Rev. 1570, 1574 (1984), reprinted in *Legal Problems, supra* note 6, at 1211.

(2)   The procedure should prevent corruption and ethical *mala fides*, even when the latter fall short of corruption and illegal activity. Another way to express this is that an important policy goal of the procedure is to prevent "back room political deals" that favor special or particular interests while defeating broader policy objectives of the ...(Community).

(3)   The procedure should enhance the perception of all parties who will be affected by a decision that they have had their chance to present information and arguments, i.e., that they have had their "day in court...."

(4)   The procedure should be perceived by the citizens at large as fair and tending to maximize the chances for a correct decision. A sense of fairness will include a desire that even weaker interests...be treated fairly....

(5)   The procedure should be reasonably efficient, that is, it should allow reasonably quick government decisions and minimize the cost both to government and to private parties of arriving at those decisions ....

(6)   The procedure should tend to maximize the likelihood that a decision will be made on a general...international basis, not catering particularly to special interests. In other words, the procedure should be designed so that government officials can realistically be assisted in "fending off" special interests that conflict with the general good of the...[Community].

(7)   The procedure must fit into the overall constitutional system[s] of the societ[ies] concerned and be consistent with the policy goals underpinning [those]constitutional system[s].

(8)   Predictability and stability of decisions are important values. Predictability of decisions, whether based on precedent, statutory formulas, or something else, enables private parties and their counselors (lawyers, economists, and politicians) to calculate generally the potential or lack of potential for a favorable decision under each of a variety of different regulatory systems . . . .[67]

To the extent that the framers of the Treaty of Chaguaramas and the State Parties thereto have agreed to establish a structure of unlimited duration, with discrete powers, rights, and duties, they have decided to set up a legal order separate and distinct from the existing sovereignties. They have

---

67. *Legal Problems, supra* note 6, at 1211-12.

volitionally ceded aspects of existing sovereignty in a discrete number of areas. Even prior to the elaboration of the Revised Treaty, what they had not done, however, is follow through and define the full external contours of the new legal order; nor had they decided on certain critical internal facets incorporating elements of the rule-based approach set out above.[68] This realization has finally dawned on the leadership of the Community.

The premier regional integration arrangement, the EU, had to face problems relating to "legal vagrancy" on the part of the Member States, even while it was instituted as a supranational entity. The EU, at that time the European Communities, had in place from the outset institutions that would ensure that there would be no faltering. The European Court of Justice stated in *Costa v. E.N.E.L.*:

> By contrast with ordinary international treaties, the EEC Treaty has created its own legal system which, on the entry into force of the treaty, became an integral part of the legal systems of the Member States and which their courts are bound to apply. By creating a Community of unlimited duration, having…powers stemming from a limitation of sovereignty or a transfer of powers from the States to the Community, the Member States have limited their sovereign rights and have thus created a body of law which binds both their nationals and themselves.[69]

Supranationality has not been a feature of the Caribbean Community, but there are treaty rules that have purported to bind CARICOM nationals. A prime example of this is Article 84(3) of the Revised Treaty, formerly Article 14(6) of the Annex to the original Treaty of Chaguaramas,[70] which deals, in the context of Community Rules of Origin, with situations where there is an interruption with supply or an inadequacy of raw materials and the manufacturer wishes to obtain extra-regional supplies. There is a requirement that "he [the manufacturer] shall so inform the competent authority" of his country,[71] who then takes the steps necessary to have the Secretary-General act.[72] This is a perfect legal duty which, in a strict jurisprudential sense, requires nothing more to give it legal effect. Sovereign States have always negotiated and will always negotiate treaties with provisions that have self-

---

68. Cf. *supra* note 24.
69 *Flaminio Costa v. E.N.E.L.*, Case 6/64, [1964] ECR 585, [1964] 1 C.M.L.R. 425. It should be noted that although the Member States have limited their own sovereign rights, they have done so within stipulated fields. The process has now reached the stage of political union.
70. See Revised Treaty, *supra* note 2, art. 84(3).
71. See id.
72. Id.

executing effect, legal positivists notwithstanding. The current leadership of the Community has now accepted that the growth and development of the Community and the very survival of their countries require the volitional cession of elements of sovereignty to the regional "pool." This becomes even more necessary as powerful extra-regional forces increasingly attempt to erode that sovereignty.[73]

Along with the foregoing change of attitude, there is a need for the Community to recognize that for the movement to progress, rules of public international law and international trade and economic law must occupy pride of place in their interaction.[74] To the extent that the thrust toward the Single Market and Economy incorporates the creation of executive, judicial, and administrative structures, implications not yet properly understood by some are involved. The changes will pose challenges. Rather than be frightened by these changes, policy makers and technocrats alike should invest intellectual capital and so create a situation allowing for the new institutions to make rules and take decisions which will give flesh to the "skeletal" Body of Community Law, which has hitherto existed but has been malnourished for thirty years.

That "Body of Community Law" will require certain supporting sources to which we now turn. The following list incorporates eligible "candidates" around which the law will develop based upon sources of Caribbean Community law:[75]

- The Treaty of Chaguaramas, its Annex, and its Protocols;

- Rules and principles of General International Law;

- Rules and principles of International Trade and Economic Law, particularly as evidenced in the GATT, the WTO, and where applicable, the practice of other Regional Economic Groupings;

- International Treaties validly concluded by the Community;

---

73. Significant sections of this Article draw on previously published and unpublished works by the present Author. See generally Sheldon A. McDonald, 'Signposts to the Development of Judicial Institutions in the Caribbean Community: The Referral Procedure of the Agreement Establishing the Caribbean Court of Justice', in CARICOM Secretariat, 2001 *Issues and Perspectives* 25-41 [hereinafter Signposts]; 'CARICOM and the New Millennium: Dispute Settlement Put Right' (2000) (unpublished, on file with author).

74. This need has been recognized by the Expert Group of Heads of Government and the Legal Affairs Committee.

75. The list includes elements which may not be formally deemed "sources." However, to the extent that they will serve to buttress the formal sources, they will be useful to the tribunal.

- Opinions of the Legal Affairs Committee;

- Instruments, Regulations, and Procedures validly adopted by Community Organs, Subsidiary Bodies and Institutions;

- Decisions of the Organs, Subsidiary Bodies, and Institutions of the Community going back as far as the Caribbean Free Trade Area ("CARIFTA");

- State practice (of Members), particularly as evidenced in bilateral trade and economic agreements between themselves and with third States or groups of third States;

- General constitutional and legal principles and fundamental rights upon which the municipal legal orders of the Member States are built;

- Determinations by the Caribbean Court of Justice and other dispute resolution bodies charged with making final determination of issues, for example, the Competition Commission and Arbitration Panels;

- Legislative, regulatory, and administrative decisions of Member States that have legal effect, but also fall within the sphere of operation of the Treaty;

- Judicial decisions of municipal tribunals impacting on provisions in the Treaty but not purporting to declare on the validity thereof, or on decisions of Organizations, Subsidiary Bodies, and Institutions of the Community.

These sources, together with an enforcement mechanism, are necessary to:

(1) protect the organization, its agents and persons entitled through them;

(2) give effect to non-political interpretation and application of the Treaty and other Community decisions;

(3) make legal determinations concerning breaches of the outputs of the decision-making structures;

(4) examine the vires of acts of the Community Institutions;

(5) the settlement of all germane disputes;

(6) establish the legal parameters of the relationship between the Community (and its Institutions) and Member States, as well as the relationship between both of these and natural and legal persons (Community nationals);

(7)   generally, control the acts of the organization and the legal limits to its power vis-à-vis the sovereignty of its members.[76]

In resolving disputes within the Community, all of the mechanisms involved, whether it be the Conference, the COTED, Arbitration Panels, Conciliation Commissions, the Competition Commission, or the Caribbean Court of Justice, will have to bear in mind two critical factors. The first is the primacy of Community Law, and the second turns on the interface between that law and the General Constitutional and legal principles and Fundamental Rights upon which the municipal legal orders of the Member States are built. This is natural given the fact that outside of flagrant breaches of treaty or other obligations, many disputes will turn on the manner in which, or the procedures by which, Members States give effect to their obligations. This will operate at three levels of interaction:

i.   Member States *inter se*;

ii.   Member States – Community Organs and Bodies; and

iii. Member States – natural and legal persons.

At the level of disputes between Community Organs and Bodies, and disputes between these entities and natural and legal persons, the issues may be no less complex, but they are susceptible to the application of the more generalized sources of law. However, it remains arguable that wherever and whenever disputes involving natural and legal persons arise, internal legal and constitutional principles and issues of fundamental rights are always raised appropriately. An analysis of how these matters were treated at an earlier stage of the development of the European Community may be of value to present efforts. The European Court of Justice's judgments in several cases are perhaps the easiest way to tackle that analysis.

The Court has always taken the view that fundamental rights constitute an integral part of the general principles which it is bound to uphold.[77] The juridical basis for the adoption of these principles derives from the long-standing practice of international tribunals to draw upon, as a source of law, general principles. It was not supposed that the new legal order of the European Communities wished to exclude this inherent interpretational tool. The Treaty of Rome implies the contrary, since Article 164 asserts that the Court shall, in interpreting the Treaty, ensure that "the law is observed."[78] In addition, Article

---

76. See *Brownlie, supra* note 10, at 680-89.

77. See *Nold v. Commission*, Case 4/73, [1974] E.C.R. 491, [1974] 2 C.M.L.R. 338.

78. See Treaty establishing the European Economic Community, Mar. 25, 1957, art. 164, 298 U.N.T.S. 11 [hereinafter EEC Treaty].

173 mentions "any rule of law" as a ground for invalidating acts of the Community.[79] Furthermore, Article 215, dealing with the non-contractual liability of the Community, sets up as a criterion the determination of such liability in accordance with "the general principles common to the laws of Member States."[80] It is concluded that given the essentially similar evolution of the legal orders in the Western European State System, a clear presumption therefore obtains that the general principles of municipal law is a source of Community Law.

D. The Principles Elaborated

1. Proportionality

In the words of the ECJ, this principle means that "the individual should not have his freedom of action limited beyond the degree necessary for the public interest."[81] Thus, a provision of a regulation requiring forfeiture of a security for any failure to perform a contract, irrespective of the gravity of the breach, was struck down.[82] The tribunal held that the penalty must be "commensurate" with the degree of failure to implement the obligations. Similarly, acts of Member States designed to implement treaty provisions, or secondary legislation, can also be struck down. This was particularly the case with derogation on provisions dealing with quantitative restrictions or their equivalent, Article 36. The ECJ has made it clear on a number of occasions that under any one of the heads, the measure must be proportionate to the mischief being sought to be corrected, and also, that where other measures can achieve the same results, derogation will not be allowed. The same approach was adopted in respect of Article 48(3) derogation concerning the free movement of workers. Thus in *Rutili*[83] and *Bouchereau*,[84] the Court insisted that the fundamental rule in Article 48 can only be avoided where there is a "genuine and sufficiently serious threat to the requirements of public policy."[85]

---

79. Id. art. 173.
80. Id. art. 215.
81. *Internationale Handelsgesellschaft mbH v. Einfuhr- und Vorratsstelle für Getreide und Futtermittel*, Case 11/70, [1970] E.C.R. 1125, 1127.
82. See *Atalanta Amsterdam BV v. Produktschap voor Vee en Vlees*, Case 240/78, [1979] E.C.R. 2137.
83. *Rutili v. Ministre de l'interieur*, Case 36/75, [1975] E.C.R. 1219.
84. *Regina v. Bouchereau*, Case 30/77, [1977] E.C.R. 1999, 2014, [1977] 2 C.M.L.R. 800, 825.
85. Id.

2. Legal Certainty and Legitimate Expectations

This principle requires that subjects of the legal system should not be placed in a position where they are uncertain as to their rights or their obligations. In *Gondrand Freres*,[86] it was decided that ambiguity or lack of clarity of measures imposing charges was to be decided in favor of the taxpayer. On the other hand, it has also been held that the principle applied in favor of Member States as well, where the latter had incurred expenditure in legitimate anticipation of financial aid from the Community. This has implications in the implementation of Chapter Seven of the Revised Treaty, particularly Article 158 establishing The Development Fund.[87] This principle also operates to preclude legislative and administrative measures taking effect without publication. Note should be taken, however, of the judgment in *Decker*, where the position was taken that a measure can have retroactive application in the exceptional circumstances if the objective to be achieved so requires and the legitimate expectations of the parties concerned are observed.[88] However, upon the special pleading of several countries, the Court in *Defrenne v. Sabena* slightly reversed itself, holding that Article 119 of the Treaty relating to non-discrimination had direct effect and could not be applied retroactively.[89] The case was one in which any other result could have led to catastrophic consequences for the economies of some Member States.

3. Equality

This principle obviously requires that differential treatment in comparable situations be based on objective factors. This has been held to be one of the fundamental principles of the Community's Civil Service Establishment. The equality principle also has implications for gender and other forms of discrimination and provisions impacting on treatment of workers discussed elsewhere in this Article.

4. Fundamental Rights

In the first place, the European Court of Justice has made reference to the European Convention on Human Rights.[90] In *Internationale Handelsgesellschaft*,

---

86. *Administration des douanes v. Société anonyme Gondrand Freres*, Case 169/80, [1981] E.C.R. 1931.
87. See *Federal Republic of Germany and Bundesanstalt für Arbeit v. Commission of the European Communities*, Case 44/81, [1982] E.C.R. 1885.
88. See *Weingut Gustav Decker KG v. Hauptzollamt Landau*, Case 99/78, [1979] E.C.R. 101.
89. See *Defrenne v. Sabena Airlines*, Case 43/75, [1976] 1 E.C.R. 455, 2 C.M.L.R. 98 (1976).
90. See, e.g., *Stauder v. City of Ulm - Sozialamt*, Case 29/69, [1969] E.C.R. 419, [1970] C.M.L.R. 112 (1970).

the tribunal rejected the contention that a Community act could be impugned for inconsistency with even the most fundamental tenet of national constitutional law.[91] However, the Court also held that:

> an examination should be made as to whether or not any analogous guarantee inherent in Community law has been disregarded. In fact, respect for fundamental rights forms an integral part of the general principles of law protected by the Court of Justice. The protection of such rights, whilst inspired by the constitutional traditions common to the Member States, must be ensured within the framework of the structure and objectives of the Community.[92]

Thus, while *Stauder* confirmed the existence of these rights, the latter judgment identified their primary source as the municipal constitutional system. The ECJ, like the European Court of Human Rights, tends towards what the latter has termed an "autonomous concept." Although the source may be national law, generalized application – in the Community context – requires that the judicial authority ensure uniformity.

The Court has also spoken approvingly of other principles of law such as due process and the right to a proper defense, and in a major decision, it upheld the confidentiality of communication between lawyer and client.[93]

5. The Supremacy of Community Law

The English scholar, Lawrence Collins, makes an interesting summary of the bases of the supremacy of Community Law derived from the case law of the ECJ. His nine-point summary is as follows:

1. Community law confers rights on individuals which national courts are bound to enforce and protect.

2. Municipal legislation cannot prevail over Community law, no matter which came first in time.

3. The efficacy of Community law cannot vary from one Member State to another.

4. Member States cannot take or maintain in force, measures that are liable to impair the useful effect of the Treaty.

5. Member States cannot give authoritative rulings [by legislation or otherwise] on the interpretation of Community Regulations.

---

91. See *Internationale Handelsgesellschaft mbH*, [1970] E.C.R. at 1127.
92. Id.
93. See *AM & S Europe Ltd. v. Commission of the European Communities*, Case 155/79, [1982] E.C.R. 1575.

6. Community law cannot be tested in municipal courts for compliance with the constitutions of Member States.

7. Member States cannot remove from ordinary courts, the power to apply Community law.

8. Where the Court declares the legislation of a Member State to be incompatible with Community law, the competent authorities of the State are under a duty to amend or repeal the offending act and its courts are under a duty to ensure the ECJ's judgment is complied with.[94]

9. Member States cannot excuse their non-performance of Treaty obligations by reliance on their domestic constitutions.[95]

III. The CCJ as the Judicial Organ of the Community

Perhaps without appreciating the juridical and legal significance of their actions, the Conference of Heads of Government of the Caribbean Community made the then Caribbean Court of Appeal, which was to be established by the Organization as the final instance tribunal for all of the Member States, the judicial organ of the Community. This is the effect of the decision taken at the meeting of the Conference of Heads of Government in 1988.

In 1970, the Organization of Commonwealth Caribbean Bar Association had recommended a Caribbean Court of Appeal. A Consultative Committee established under its auspices confirmed that support and proposed an original jurisdiction for the said court in treaty matters falling under the Dickensen Bay Agreement Establishing the Caribbean Free Trade Area. Also in 1970, the Conference of Heads of Government of the Commonwealth Caribbean (the precursor to the Caribbean Community), adopted a resolution calling for the establishment of such a court.

The Conference paused in the drive to establish the judicial tribunal until the establishment in 1989 of the West Indian Commission, which was designed to comprehensively review the integration movement and propose measures to ensure its growth and development in the then-changing international political, economic, and legal orders. In 1992, that body would recommend that the Community establish a Caribbean Supreme

---

94. The process has reached the stage where financial penalties now attach to Member States for infringement of sections of the Treaties.

95. Lawrence Collins, *European Community Law in the United Kingdom* 11-12 (1984). Collins appears at times to be nostalgic, anticipating the lost of the supposed English "distinctiveness" and yet unreconciled that the U.K. would be in Europe "forever." Id.

Court, with both appellate and original jurisdiction. The new judicial tribunal would be considered as an "autonomous body" of the Community – its judicial organ. Those persons who are timorous about describing the CCJ as the judicial organ of the Community only apparently are rescued by the fact that the two newest Members, Suriname and Haiti are not common law jurisdictions. The rescue however, is more apparent than real. As will be seen, the legal and political schema around the Court confirms its roles as the judicial organ.

The appellate jurisdiction of the Court notwithstanding, the institution will play a pivotal role in re-shaping the socio-economic landscape of the Members of the Community as a result of the judgments, opinions, and orders it will make in the context of the Single Market and Economy. The common law systems will benefit from the flow-over effect of decisions made in the treaty context involving disputes in which the civil law countries are litigants, given the binding effect of the judgments. Similarly, the civil law systems of the Community will not escape that flow of the regional common law jurisprudence of the appellate court into the municipal domain, particularly in such areas as human rights. In fact, the Chief Justice of the Eastern Caribbean Supreme Court,[96] His Lordship, Sir Denis Byron, is already on the record predicting that the CCJ will be the biggest single contributor to the harmonization of the practice and application of law in the Member States of the Community.

Furthermore, the Project Coordinating Unit for the Establishment of the CCJ has sponsored a process of engagement between the legal academic community of the University of the West Indies and the University systems of Haiti and Suriname on the requirements of legal education in the new dispensation. The Legal Affairs Committee has also received proposals from the Council of Legal Education on these matters. These steps form a logical part of the process of the fashioning of an indigenous jurisprudence. The need for a sea change in the legal and jurisprudential approaches to integration has been finally accepted at the highest level of the Community.

The Rose Hall Declaration emanating from the Twenty-Fourth Meeting of the Conference of Heads of Government, adopted on the Thirtieth Anniversary of the Community, July 4, 2003, in Montego Bay, Jamaica, recognizes the

---

96. The Eastern Caribbean Supreme Court includes the national High Courts of nine Eastern Caribbean States and a single Court of Appeal for the States, thereby giving those States harmony in judicial interpretation.

need to change direction.[97] It tackles the issue of supranationality by disclaiming any pretense at achieving it, given not only the fact that CARICOM is a "Community of Sovereign States" but also the expedience of the movement towards regional integration proceeding in that "political and juridical context."[98] However, that having being said, the instrument speaks of the

> development of a system of mature regionalism in which critical policy decisions of the Community taken by Heads of Government, or by other Organs of the Community, will have the force of law throughout the Region as a result of the operation of domestic legislation and the Revised Treaty of Chaguaramas appropriately revised, and the *authority of the Caribbean Court of Justice in its Original Jurisdiction* – taking into account the constitutional provisions of the Member States.[99]

CARICOM will be doing no more or no less than the "parent" of the constitutional law and practice of the majority of its Member States, the United Kingdom, which was constrained, upon accession to the European Communities, to enact legislation giving domestic legal effect to Community Law, with all its supranationality.[100]

In arriving at this position in 2003, the Conference was merely reminding itself (indirectly) of its earlier decision made in 1999. This decision directed the Secretariat to consider measures of ensuring the effective integration of Suriname and Haiti – with their civil law systems – into the Community, particularly as regards the effective participation of both of these countries in the CCJ.[101] That decision was arrived at after the Conference underscored the "centrality of the Caribbean Court of Justice in the institutional structures of the Community, including its importance to the successful functioning of the CARICOM Single Market and Economy."[102]

---

97. The Rose Hall Declaration on "Regional Governance and Integrated Development" Adopted on the Occasion of the Thirtieth Anniversary of the Caribbean Community (CARICOM) at the Twenty-Fourth Meeting of the Conference of Heads of Government of CARICOM, July 2-5, 2003, available at http://www.caricom.org/archives/rosehalldeclaration.htm.

98. Id. art. A, para. 1.

99. Id. art. A, para. 2 (emphasis added).

100. See the discussion on the United Kingdom's European Communities Act, 1972, *infra* note 150 and accompanying text.

101. See Communiqué of the Seventh Special Meeting of the Conference of Heads of Government of the Caribbean Community (CARICOM), Chaguaramas, Trinidad and Tobago, October 26-27, 1999, available at http://www.caricom.org/archives/communiques-hgc/7sphgc-1999-communique.htm. This was also the meeting that decided to set up the Preparatory Committee for the Establishment of the Caribbean Court of Justice. See id.

102. Id.

Although it is very clear that the CCJ has to be the judicial organ of the Community, the issue has nonetheless been actively debated at the technical level. Indeed, there had to be a bifurcation, with respect to the Revised Treaty and the Agreement Establishing the Caribbean Court of Justice (the "CCJ Agreement"),[103] precisely because of the *sui generis* nature of the Court.

All the rights and obligations under the Revised Treaty fall upon "Member States of the Community." These are set out in Article 3.[104] In the definitional Article 1, the first juridical separation of the institutions directly constituted under and regulated by the Revised Treaty and other bodies occurs.[105] "Agreement" is defined as "the Agreement Establishing the Caribbean Court of Justice," and concomitantly, "Court" is so defined.[106] The Court, while receiving its juridical empowerment under the constituent instrument of the Community, will be established under and regulated by a separate international instrument. A similar situation arises with the CARICOM Regional Organization for Standards and Quality ("CROSQ"), which is provided for by Article 67(5) of the Revised Treaty, but came into being by way of an Inter-Governmental Agreement. On the other hand, the Organs of the Community, the Competition Commission, and other entities with important functions including actions on the international legal plane, are all directly regulated under the Revised Treaty.

Contrary to an argument which would place them as being completely distinct from the treaty-created and regulated entities, it is closer to reality that given the tasks entrusted to the CCJ and CROSQ, as well the political context in which they are being established, the Member States accepted the advice that they be given distinct juridical personality and legal capacities. In terms of the CCJ, the need for this separation is also related to the issue of membership. Article 3(2) of the Revised Treaty allows membership into the Community of "any other State or Territory of the Caribbean Region that is, in the opinion of the Conference, able and willing to exercise the rights and assume the obligations of Membership."[107] However, in the case of the Court,

---

103. Agreement Establishing the Caribbean Court of Justice, Feb. 14, 2000, available at http://www.caricom.org/archives/agreement-ccj.htm (entered into force on July 23, 2003 upon the deposit of the Instrument of ratification by Guyana) [hereinafter CCJ Agreement]. Earlier, Saint Lucia had ratified at the Twenty-Third Meeting of the Conference, early July, 2003, and, shortly thereafter, the Barbados followed suit. Entry into force occurred pursuant to Article XXV.

104. See Revised Treaty, *supra* note 2, art. 3.

105. See id. art. 1.

106. Id.

107. Id. art. 3(2).

membership is more restricted. Given its *sui generis* nature, a State or Territory may be "able and willing to exercise the rights and assume the obligations of membership," but they still have another threshold to cross. In the words of Article II of the CCJ Agreement, membership to the Court is open to any member of the Community as well as "[a]ny other Caribbean country, which is invited by the Conference to become a Party to this Agreement."[108]

The Conference may, in its wisdom, invite a Caribbean country to become a member of the Court, even if that country has no interest in becoming a member of the Community. This is not as incongruous as it may appear. A country with which the Community has extensive bilateral trade and economic interaction could conceivably think it appropriate to become a part of the CCJ Agreement and thus avail itself of an authoritative and determinative dispute settlement regime without taking on all the obligations of membership in the Community. Conversely, a Commonwealth Caribbean country or Territory may not be able to exercise the rights and assume the obligations of membership of the Community, but may find it convenient or may be allowed to participate in the appellate jurisdiction of the Court.[109] The invitation to join would thus be appropriate in both circumstances.

However, while all of the Member States "agree that they recognize as compulsory *ipso facto* and without special agreement, the original jurisdiction of the court referred to in Article 211,"[110] it will be only those Member States Contracting Parties to the Agreement that will have *locus standi*. Article 211 states:

1. Subject to this Treaty, the Court shall have compulsory and exclusive jurisdiction to hear and determine disputes concerning the interpretation and application of the Treaty, including:
   a. disputes between the Member States parties to this Agreement;
   b. disputes between Member states parties to the Agreement and the Community;
   c. referrals from national courts of the Member States parties to the Agreement;
   d. application by persons in accordance with Article 222, concerning the interpretation and application of this Treaty.

---

108. CCJ Agreement, *supra* note 103, art. II.
109. The CCJ Agreement carries its own discrete set of rights and obligations, for example, those relating to the financing of the entity and enforcement of the judgments, orders, etc. of the Court. See id. art. XXVI-II.
110. Revised Treaty, *supra* note 2, art. 211.

Concomitantly, in the CCJ Agreement, it is stipulated that the various heads of jurisdiction set out above can only be accessed by or utilized against Contracting Parties to the Agreement.[111] Furthermore, in respect to appellate jurisdiction, which is not addressed in the Revised Treaty, but in the CCJ Agreement, it is stipulated that "the Court is a superior Court of Record with such jurisdiction and powers as are conferred on it by this Agreement or by the Constitution or any other law of a Contracting Party."[112]

The juridical distinction drawn between Membership in the Community and participation in the Court regime does in fact permeate the latter. The fact is that the initial function of the tribunal in the appellate role within a State system where the common law is the dominant tradition has been augmented by an international dispute settlement competence. There are two Member States that have distinct legal systems and that will not use the appellate jurisdiction of the Court, and even some of the Commonwealth Caribbean Members of the Community (even initially) may opt not to adhere to that municipal jurisdiction. This is a quintessential sovereign function. Further proof of the separation is to be seen in the fact that the right of audience before the Court is limited to practitioners duly admitted to practice law in the courts of Contracting Parties to the CCJ Agreement,[113] so that legal practitioners from the Member States not Parties to the CCJ Agreement are excluded, unless and until they are admitted to the bar of a Party.

The Revised Treaty is the overriding instrument constituting the Community. The Single Market and Economy is integral thereto. The CCJ is crucial for the functioning of the latter, and so all Member States have to contract into the CCJ – in its original jurisdiction – as the judicial organ of the Community. This objective is secured by way of Chapter 9 and specifically Articles 211 to 222. This binding power *erga omnes*, is reinforced by the fact that by Article 221 decisions of the Court will constitute *stare decisis*.[114] This is yet another innovation in the regime to which we will return. Article 221 provides: "Judgments of the Court shall constitute legally binding precedents for parties before the Court unless such judgments have been revised in accordance with Article 219."[115] As will be seen, when this provision and the *non liquet* rule is discussed, the fashioning of the law in the new order will inescapably have an impact across its two jurisdictions and two legal systems,

---

111. CCJ Agreement, *supra* note 103, art. XII.
112. Id. art. XXV, para. 1.
113. Id. art. XXIX.
114. See Revised Treaty, *supra* note 2, art. 221.
115. Id.

particularly if one accepts that issues of social and economic rights cannot be seen as being distinct in countries such as Haiti and Jamaica.

Hence, while the CCJ Agreement contains the substantive provisions of the appellate jurisdiction, for the purpose of discussing the CCJ as the judicial organ of the Community, that instrument, at this time, is really more in the nature of a statute. If the time ever arrives where all the Members of CARICOM determine that they wish to have another tier in their judicial hierarchy and accord that role to the CCJ, then it will become the complete judicial organ as envisaged by the West Indian Commission and the OCCBA's Consultative Committee. Due to sensitivity over the issue of sovereignty this kind of approach is often not candidly analysed.

Another reason for this "discussion-deficit" has to do with insulating the Court from the perception or possibility of any kind of external interference, particularly political interference. In fact, the CCJ Agreement is completely inviolate in that regard. From the present perspective, the correct approach is not to disclaim the central role of the tribunal, but rather to take reinforcing measures if these are required. We will look at the practice elsewhere.

Other integration regimes have established regional courts and have explicitly named them as the judicial organ. The premiere integration *schema*, the European Community, organized it in the following way in the Treaty of Rome:

> The tasks entrusted to the Community shall be carried out by the following institutions:
>
> > European Parliament,
> > Council,
> > Commission,
> > Court of Justice,
> > Court of Auditors.
>
> Each institution shall act within the limits of the powers conferred upon it by this Treaty.[116]

There is no scope for the Parliament, the Council, or the Commission to issue instructions to the Court, as such actions would be *ultra vires* of the "limits of the powers conferred on them." The Conference of Heads of Government is the Supreme Organ of the Community, pursuant to Article 12 of the Revised Treaty, and has the authority to determine the policy directions of the Community.[117]

---

116. EEC Treaty, *supra* note 78, art. 4.1.
117. See Revised Treaty, *supra* note 2, art. 12, para. 2.

However, given the fact that the rule of law and the doctrine of the separation of powers are living features within the constitutional orders of all the Members of the Community, it would be improper to infer that the above competence would be used by the Conference to influence the CCJ. On the other hand, no matter how practically distant, the theoretically legal possibility does exist for such interference. But that lacuna can be closed. The European Community precedent set out above is largely followed in respect to regional Courts of the following: The European Free Trade Area; The Andean Community; The Common Market of Eastern and Southern Africa ("COMESA"); and the Economic Community of West African States ("ECOWAS"). While the constituent instrument of the first three makes no attempt to specifically insulate the judicial tribunal, the ECOWAS Revised Treaty does: Article 6 sets out the institution of the Community, and paragraph 2 therein requires each to "perform their functions and act within the limits of the powers conferred on them by this Treaty and the Protocols relating thereto."[118]

However, the architects of the regime did not believe that the judicial institution was sufficiently insulated. In consequence, one finds in Article 15 of the ECOWAS Treaty, on the Establishment and Functions of the Court, the following stipulation in paragraph 3: "The Court of Justice shall carry out the functions assigned to it independently of the Member States and the Institutions of the Community."[119] This provision provides one way in which the lacuna in the CARICOM regime can be closed.

The Revised Treaty provides fertile ground for the CCJ to develop the indigenous body of Community law that is so often spoken about. Clearly with respect to trade in goods and services generally, the free movement of capital, competition policy, inter-institutional disputes, disputes between Member States and the Organs and Institutions and disputes between regional organizations established by Inter-Governmental Agreements and the Community *qua* Community counsel will plead, and the bench will have recourse to, the sources of law discussed above. In respect to competition policy, the Revised Treaty provides a discrete regime in Chapter 8, which involves a regional quasi-judicial Competition Commission and national authorities. It is obvious however, that issues, particularly at the municipal level, will reach the Court either by way of the referral procedure or at the

---

118. Economic Community of West African States: Revised Treaty, July 24, 1993, art. 6, 35 I.L.M. 660, 668 [hereinafter ECOWAS].
119. Id. art. 15, para. 3.

behest of natural and legal persons seeking to have their rights vindicated pursuant to Article 222.

On the other hand, there are three specific situations where the Court is empowered directly in this matter. First, in respect of Determination of Anti-Competitive Business Conduct regulated by Article 175, the Commission is authorized to investigate claims and, where appropriate, issue instructions for corrective action. Paragraph 11 brings in the judicial body to give teeth to that instruction: "If the enterprise cannot comply with the time period specified [in the instruction] and fails to inform the Commission, the Commission may apply to the Court for an order."[120] The enterprise affected may take the view that the Commission is acting unjustly. In that situation, a party "which is aggrieved by a determination of the Commission under paragraph 4 of Article 174 in any matter may apply to the Court for a review of that determination."[121]

There are also situations where the Commission, *proprio motu*, decides to investigate anti-competitive business conduct.[122] The Council for Trade and Economic Development ("COTED") is given the authority to settle issues of differences between the Commission and the Member State. However, even in this situation, the exclusive and compulsory jurisdiction of the Court is retained: "Nothing in this Article shall prejudice the right of the Member State to initiate proceedings before the Court at any time."[123]

There is a cluster of issues that, although dealt with in the Revised Treaty, require action thereon either by the Community, Member States, or a combination of both. Disputes here will turn on whether these entities have or have not carried out their duties. Some of these issues include Intellectual Property Rights and the Management and Utilization of Natural Resources, including maritime resources. Invariably, the regime will have to establish some sort of Human Rights regime as well, and the Court will sit automatically at its apex.

There is one matter that has to be addressed early, and the Revised Treaty as well as the CCJ Agreement may need to be amended by way of a protocol to address this matter: Public Servants in the Member States have recourse to municipal courts for judicial review of administrative actions in relation to their conditions of service. International public servants in the pay of the United Nations have recourse to its Administrative Tribunal. However, servants

---

120. Revised Treaty, *supra* note 2, art. 175, para. 11.
121. Id. art. 175, para. 12.
122. See generally id. art. 176.
123. Id. art. 176, para. 6.

of the Caribbean Community do not have this right, and they are precluded from taking their case to municipal courts. The regime must at some time – preferably sooner rather than later – be adjusted to incorporate, within the jurisdiction of the CCJ, the same empowerment that is given to the ECJ by the Treaty of Rome: "The Court of Justice shall have jurisdiction in any disputes between the Community and its servants within the limits and under the conditions laid down in the Staff Regulations or the Conditions of employment."[124]

Another possible expansion of the jurisdiction of the Court, which again could be adapted from the EU, is the empowerment to accept specially agreed requests from Member States to settle disputes that relate to matters contained in the Revised Treaty, but that are of a strictly bilateral nature and fall within matters reserved for the Member States themselves. Issues which come to mind include maritime delimitation and the utilization of natural resources. These issues are addressed with the Industrial Policy Chapter, and they are related to international obligations the Member States have under international law, particularly the United Nations Convention on the Law of the Sea, and the Agreement on Highly Migratory and Straddling Fish Stocks. There have been frequent disputes between Member States over both issues. The Treaty of Rome, in Article 82, provides as follows: "The Court of Justice shall have jurisdiction in any dispute between Member States which relates to the subject matter of this Treaty if the dispute is submitted to it under a special agreement between the parties."[125]

The disputes that have arisen and are amenable to being settled in this way have often threatened to rupture relations between Members of the Community, and bilateral negotiations have often proven incapable to breaking the impasse. It is submitted that the Member States concerned would have confidence in their judicial tribunal to find the means of resolving these issues.

An emerging energy issue that is likely to engage the CCJ very early on involves the issue of national treatment and non-discrimination in respect of access to and pricing of natural resources as these relate to energy within the context of the CSME. There is a disagreement between two Member States regarding access to and pricing of liquid natural gas ("LNG"), or the natural gas that goes into making liquid natural gas, that is being purchased by a member state from another member state that produces natural gas. As the General Counsel of the CARICOM Secretariat has expressed it:

---

124. See EEC Treaty, *supra* note 78, art. 236.
125. Id. art. 239.

A regional energy policy is widely regarded as critical but the interests of Member States do not necessarily converge. For energy exporting countries, expansion in natural gas output (and high export prices) is anticipated to have positive impacts of seismic proportions in relation to such key macro-economic variables as GDP, Balance of Payments, government revenue and expenditure, and industrial competitiveness. For energy importing countries, access to regional natural gas is welcomed as reducing dependency on imported oil by diversification of energy consumption, protecting the economy from the destabilizing impact of oil price volatility and, generally, enhancing the competitiveness of the protective sector. Industrial competitiveness is among the most immediate concern. Energy is a significant cost component in the manufacturing process. Access by the productive sector in one Member State to natural gas at lower net back prices than is available to the productive sector in other Member States, has been claimed to have had a devastating impact upon the manufacturing industry and balance of payment profile in many of the first State's traditional trading partners within the Community.[126]

IV. The Jurisdictional and Institutional Distinctiveness of the Caribbean Court of Justice

The features that make the Caribbean Court of Justice distinctive are:

- the unique nature of its jurisdiction;
- the *non liquet* rule;
- the role of the doctrine of *stare decisis* and precedent in the original jurisdiction;
- *locus standi* for natural and legal persons;
- the referral procedure;
- the advisory opinion procedure;
- the modality utilized for appointing the Judges;
- the modality utilized for the appointment of the President;
- sources from which the Judges may be drawn;
- mode of financing the Court;

---

126. Advisory Opinion on National Treatment and Non-discrimination in respect of access to, and pricing of natural resources as these relate to energy in the context of the CSME, CARICOM Secretariat, October 2003 [hereinafter Advisory Opinion]; see also David Renwick, 'Pricing LNG Within CARICOM', *Trinidad Guardian*, Nov. 30, 2003, available at http://petroleumworld.com/storyTT194.htm (last visited Feb. 5, 2004) (reporting on the Jamaican position on the Advisory Opinion as it relates to natural gas pricing by Trinidad and Tobago).

- the peripatetic nature of the Court; and
- compliance with Judgments and Orders.

In terms of the jurisdictional distinctiveness, significant elements of this have been discussed above. The Revised Treaty empowers the institution in terms of its original jurisdiction. Articles 211-222 are repeated, with the consequential changes, in the CCJ Agreement. However, to demonstrate that both jurisdictions of equal importance to the Community and to the Member States concerned, Article III of the latter establishes the Court with:

(a) Original jurisdiction in accordance with the provisions of Part II, and

(b) Appellate jurisdiction in accordance with the provisions of Part III.[127]

In the case of both jurisdictions, "[t]he decisions of the Court shall be final."[128]

While in the common law context, *stare decisis* and precedent are the norm, it is acknowledged that international tribunals are given to the notion of *jurisprudence constant,* although the European Court of Justice has often gone further and adopted an approach closer to the common law regime. What makes the CCJ distinctive is that the doctrines have been imported over into the international facet of its jurisdiction. This will mean, from the outset, that all Member States, Community Organs and Bodies, as well as natural and legal persons operating with the CSME, will be bound by all its judgments, orders, and will have to think twice about ignoring Advisory Opinions. The Community does not have the luxury of time for the precepts of the supremacy and uniformity of Community law to take effect. The Community is a capital-importing region, and, therefore, the need exists to create a socio-economic environment where external investors, as well as those within the Community, can have legitimate expectations as to the outcome of investment decisions.

V. *Non Liquet and Stare Decisis*

In its original jurisdiction, the law to be applied by the Court is set out in both instruments as "such rules of international law as may be applicable."[129] Within that broad rubric, it is suggested that the sources of law discussed above would form the flesh for this skeletal provision. It is noted as well that the Court would necessarily have to ascertain the domestic legal rules involved in particular situations. As in Conflict of Laws, it could be said that they

---

127. CCJ Agreement, *supra* note 103, art. III, para. 1.
128. Id. art. III, para. 2.
129. Id. art. XVII; Revised Treaty, *supra* note 2, art. 217.

would be treated as facts. However, a wider view would affirm that the Court ought to examine the last two sources set out, as well as the general constitutional and legal principles of the domestic jurisdictions involved, in order to fashion a more appropriate and progressive view of the state of international law in the particular context in which it operates. This would have the added value of strengthening the uniformity of Caribbean Community law and thus engendering greater legal certainty.

Under both the Revised Treaty and the CCJ Agreement, the Court is prohibited from refusing to determine a matter on the grounds of silence or obscurity of the law: "The Court may not bring in a *non liquet* on the ground of silence or obscurity of the law."[130] Earl Jowett notes that in the civil law systems, instead of deciding a case, the judges could, if the facts did not point to a definite conclusion, write "NL" and leave the matter for determination sometime in the future.[131] The presence of both common law and civil law systems in the legal order of the Community requires a more definitive position on this matter. In consequence, the provision barring *non liquet* from being applied was deemed to be in order. Although international law, particularly trade and economic law, has developed rapidly, there are still lacunae.

Notwithstanding such positive expectations regarding the interface between the two systems of law there remain concerns about the dilution of the civil law norms by the perceived overwhelming common law tradition of the Community. The Community's civil law countries may be only two in number, but the fact remains that there are 9 million civil law citizens in a Community of 14 million. These 9 million civil law citizens will bring with them not only different legal systems, but also new culture, new history, new national political considerations, and new economic realities and history, and this may well raise similar unnecessary alarms among the common law peoples. But the Heads of Government have resolved – by the act of welcoming Suriname and Haiti to the Community – to overcome the non-legal differences and concerns and to extract the positive benefits rather than be intimidated by the less attractive matters. It falls within the domain of the CCJ and the members of the legal fraternity who turn up to argue the matters that engage the Court to ensure that the legal diversity is not an impediment to economic (and social) cohesion but rather – and rightly so – a boon to the integration process.

At this prefatory stage, it can be safely predicted that the Court in its Appellate Jurisdiction will provide harmonization in judicial interpretation

---

130. CCJ Agreement, supra note 103, art. XVII, para. 2; Revised Treaty, *supra* note 2, art. 217, para. 2.

131. Earl Jowett, *The Dictionary of English Law* 1233 (1959).

across the Member States. This is indeed most desirable for the integration process especially in the sphere of human rights[132] and commercial transactions. In the latter sphere, it may be instructive to note that the Commonwealth Caribbean Member States have already implemented harmonized Companies legislation. However, in its Original Jurisdiction, the civil law anxiety of being overwhelmed by common law thinking is more pronounced. In a recent presentation by H.R. Lim A. Po,[133] the author prefaced his concerns from a civil law perspective in the following words:

> The principle of *non-liquet* and the doctrine of *stare decisis* are attributes of supranationality. [Another writer] has elaborated extensively on these attributes and has concluded that, in exercising original jurisdiction, these attributes appear to be open to considerably less ambiguity and speculation than in the exercise of the Court's appellate jurisdiction.

> My submission is than in the application of the principle of *non-liquet* and *stare decisis* in the jurisdiction of the Caribbean Court, differences in the legal systems of the Member States become relevant.

> There is a risk of bias in the Court for common law reasoning when filling gaps in international treaty and customary law and when applying the doctrine of *stare decisis*. *Stare decisis* is not a doctrine of civil law. Nor is it a doctrine of international law, so it would be natural for the Court to relate in its decision making to the manner in which this doctrine is applied in common law.[134]

The learned jurist continues to highlight the differences between the systems in the following words:

> Important differences are that lawyers from the civil law countries tend to be more conceptual, while lawyers from the common law countries are considered to be more pragmatic. And that priority is given to doctrine over jurisprudence in civil

---

132. This already exists among the Member States who retain the Privy Council. A recent decision of that Court extended the constitutional interpretation mechanism first implemented in the Eastern Caribbean and Belize, which held that the statutory mandatory death sentence for murder conflicted with enshrined constitutional rights. See *Spence v. The Queen* (not yet reported) April 2, 2001 (appeals taken from Saint Vincent and Saint Lucia) (Criminal Appeals Nos. 20 of 1998 and 14 of 1997); see also *Reyes v. The Queen*, 2 App. Cas. 235 (P.C. 2002) (appeal taken from Belize).

133. H.R. Lim A. Po, "Bridging the Divide:" The interface between the Civil Law system and the Common Law system, with special emphasis on the role of the CCJ, Address to the Symposium on "The Caribbean Court of Justice" in Paramaribo (Oct. 31, 2003) [hereinafter Bridging the Divide].

134. Id. at 1-2.

law; while the opposite is true in common law. Also, in civil law the legal rule has risen to a higher level of abstraction compared to common law. . . .

Civil law statutes do not provide definitions. On the other hand, the common law style of drafting emphasizes precision rather than conciseness. Common law statutes provide detailed definitions, and each specific rule sets out lengthy enumerations of specific applications or exceptions. These differences in style can also be found in international conventions. . . .

In civil law the main tasks of courts are to decide on particular cases by applying and interpreting legal norms, while in common law, courts not only decide on disputes but are also supposed to provide guidance as to how similar disputes should be settled in the future.[135]

Finally, the author correctly observes that "the growing globalization of the world economy, which is based on closer integration and cooperation among states, imposes a need for legal certainty and unification of law. This process involves further reducing differences between various legal systems and harmonization of the common law and civil law legal systems."[136]

In view of the need for clarity and predictability in the interpretation of the Revised Treaty by the sole adjudicative body, the CCJ, the framers of the treaty and the CCJ Agreement have given the States the comfort of the doctrine of *stare decisis*. Is this desirable? In a commentary on the experience of the European Court of Justice, Anthony Arnull made the following observation:

The general position may be stated very simply: the Court of Justice is not bound by its previous decisions but in practice it does not often depart from them. A doctrine of binding precedent on common law lines would have been entirely inappropriate in what was originally a court of first and last resort, many of whose decisions could only be changed by amending the Treaties, a lengthy process requiring the agreement of all Member States and ratification by each of them in accordance with their respective constitutional requirements. It was therefore imperative that the Court should have the power to change the direction of its case law and to depart from its previous decisions, particularly in cases of important constitutional implications.[137]

The learned author illustrates through a series of cases that the Court's freedom to depart from previous decisions had to be matched by the logical expectation

---

135. Id. at 2-3.
136. Id. at 4.
137. Anthony Arnull, *The European Union and its Court of Justice* 529 (1999).

that a Court of law would demonstrate consistency and reconciliation with previous decisions. Whether through the influence of common law philosophy or otherwise, the Court strived to do this with limited success. The result was an untenable situation where reference was happily made to previous decisions that explained a current view but inconsistent decisions were ignored or overlooked.[138]

Ultimately, the Court evolved to a position that Arnull describes as an "increasing sophistication … in handling its previous case law."[139] He therefore concludes,

> it also now seems to be recognized that …departures require an explanation of the cases affected in order to avoid an unacceptable degree of uncertainty about the new legal position. Where the Court declines to reverse a previous decision, it appears to accept that a detailed explanation of its reasoning may be equally necessary. It remains true that the Court does not often depart from its previous decisions. The difference is that it is now less common for the Court to ignore or misrepresent inconvenient earlier authorities.[140]

It is clear that the Caribbean Court of Justice in its original jurisdiction, through the interpretation and application of appropriate sources of law, will be exercising a critical integration function of fleshing out the practical rights and obligations of parties who appear before it. The paper rights and obligations enshrined in the Revised Treaty come alive and find true meaning in their interpretation and application. As the experience in the treatment of municipal law "ouster clauses" that sought to preclude judicial review in municipal law brings to mind, the restraint of Courts by statues is often overcome, and where necessary should be overcome. It is not suggested that judicial law-making is desirable or necessary, but it may be that in the CARICOM experience, the Revised Treaty will only bring the desired benefits to the Community if the Court's creativity is reasonably unbridled. The prohibition of the civil law concept of *non liquet* is a statutory mandate for vision and imagination.

The necessity for liberal interpretation in these circumstances may ultimately overwhelm the extent to which the pure application of *stare decisis* obtains. As Lim A. Po puts it, "one would expect situations to rise over time in which reversal of earlier rulings would be appropriate in order to ensure that the

---

138. See id. at 529-33.
139. Id. at 533.
140. Id.

Treaty would be interpreted and applied as a 'living document' that steers rather than stifles development."[141] Indeed it is clear that the CCJ may find its duty to the Community best served by adopting a "restrictive policy in the application of the doctrine of *stare decisis.*"[142]

Additionally, the theoretical fetter on judicial creativity in the Revised Treaty correctly retains for the Member States the notion, however abstract, of national sovereignty and legislative supremacy. As the Court becomes operational, however, the manner in which it balances the philosophical opposite, but equally important forces will be critical to the advancement of the integration process.

One may conclude that the philosophical chasm between an international tribunal that applies the doctrine of *stare decisis* and one that does not is not as far apart as it may first appear. The certainty that flows from consistency has been the chosen path of the European Court of Justice. Likewise, from the other direction, creativity that qualifies the rigidity of *stare decisis* is a necessity for the CCJ. It is suggested that the approach set out above could assist in the filling of these interstices that exist in the emerging body of Community law.

The Court also has discretion to apply rules of equity with the agreement of the parties to a dispute. This is set out in both the Revised Treaty and the CCJ Agreement, which provide as follows: "[t]he provisions of paragraphs (1) and (2) shall not prejudice the power of the Court to decide a dispute *ex aqueo et bueno* if the Parties so agree."[143] This power derives from the ICJ Statute Article 38 (2), and as in that instrument, this competence qualifies the duty to apply applicable rules of international law. Ian Brownlie considers that [in the case of the ICJ], "[t]he exercise of this power, which has not yet occurred, may not be easy to reconcile with the judicial character of the tribunal."[144]

While at the level of general international law, the doctrine of *stare decisis* is not formally recognized, the specialized context in which the CCJ will operate like the ECJ requires a different approach. As such, judgments of the Court will constitute precedent, pursuant to Article 221, which provides: "judgments of the Court shall constitute legally binding precedents for parties in proceedings before the Court unless such judgments have been revised in

---

141. Po, *supra* note 133, at 10.

142. Id.

143. CCJ Agreement, *supra* note 103, art. XVII, para. 3; Revised Treaty, *supra* note 2, art. 217, para. 3.

144. Brownlie, *supra* note 10, at 690.

accordance with Article 219."[145] This approach to the doctrine may seem somewhat limited. First, the precedent force of the judgment would appear to impact only upon parties in proceedings before the Court. Thus, the legislative, executive and judicial authorities of the Member States concerned will have to act accordingly. Conceivably, however, a Member State that either has not gone to Court, or has not intervened in an action may regard itself as not bound. I would suggest that this would be a narrow line of reasoning, manifesting a paucity of understanding of the wider purpose in which the tribunal is operating.

The judgment of the Court in relation to Community organs and bodies will be translated into action by decisions. These decisions bind all the Members of the Community. It is likely that a municipal court will determine a case where there is a clear precedent, as opposed to utilizing the referral process. The latter must be seen as applicable at all times, but it will be of greatest value when the municipal tribunal is unclear or in great doubt as to how it should interpret Community Law. The foregoing must be the case if the precept that the administration of justice requires that like cases be decided similarly is to be upheld. As Brown posits: "Inconsistency in judicial decisions affronts even the most elementary sense of justice. In this sense the principle of *stare decisis*, of abiding by previous decisions, figures prominently in most legal systems . . . ."[146]

The rules that have been developed around the doctrine of precedent will have to be applied creatively in the context of the CCJ. From the appellate jurisdiction perspective, it is much easier for judicial reticence to be the order of the day. The continuing legacy of the English jurisprudential tradition requires strict adherence to the doctrine. On the other hand, the Caribbean Community has two Member States, Haiti and Suriname, for which, given their civil law tradition, the doctrine of precedent is foreign. There are also other Member States within whose jurisprudential history the *Code Civile* has played a not insignificant part. As in the common law tradition, the predominant view within these jurisdictions is that judicial decisions do not constitute a formal source of law. There is no need for a judge in those countries to reconcile a new judgment with earlier ones, even if inconsistency would be avoided.

The experience of the European Court of Justice in this matter offers no straight forward conclusions for ready application in our context. The decisions

---

145. Revised Treaty, *supra* note 2, art. 221.
146. L. Neville Brown & Francis Jacobs, *The Court of Justice of the European Communities* 311 (1989).

of that tribunal are obviously authoritative, and the Court normally follows its own decisions. In addition, as Brown notes, the judgments are:

> abstract and syllogistic, rather than concrete and discursive like the typical English
> ... judgment .... Although they now sometimes refer to previous decisions which
> they are following, they rarely allude to any earlier decisions from which they may
> be departing. Their character has a decisive impact on the question of precedent.
> First, it means that the judgments often start from broad propositions of law which
> may not be intended to be taken at face value, in absolute terms, but rather to be
> refined by subsequent decisions .... Second, judgments of this kind do not easily
> lend themselves to the characteristic technique of distinguishing earlier judgments
> in the way of an English lawyer.[147]

So while the ECJ may follow its previous decisions, as it did in developing doctrines such as the direct effect of Community Law, it cannot be said that the Court regards itself as being bound by previous decisions:

> Although the English lawyers may find it strange that the Court should not
> expressly recognize that it is departing from precedent let alone give no reasons for
> doing so, the fact that it should have this freedom can be readily understood. A
> final court can only be bound by its previous decisions if the law established by
> those decisions can, in the last resort be amended by legislation. Since the decisions
> of the Court of Justice could be affected only by an amendment of the Treaties, a
> practical impossibility, it is inevitable that it should be flexible in its approach to
> precedent.[148]

The position with the Caribbean Court of Justice, with respect to its appellate jurisdiction, is that decisions there can be amended by legislative enactments within the domestic legal order of the contracting parties. On the other hand, it is indeed a "practical impossibility" to anticipate amendment of the Revised Treaty to mitigate or otherwise amend the law developed by the Court with respect to the original jurisdiction.[149] As argued above, in relation to the role of municipal law in the work of the Court, some measure of flexibility will be required.

At another level, the decisions of the courts of the Member States also figure in the matter of precedent. The fact that national law is binding upon the CCJ, as an appellate tribunal, does not preclude a synergistic relationship with Community law. Thus, national law can render assistance in the development of precedent. Constitutional principles will assist in the

---

147. Id. at 312-13.
148. Id. at 314-15.
149. Id. at 315.

fashioning of the law, which itself will have the status of precedent. Additionally, municipal law, particularly the decisions of tribunals, will obviously figure where questions of the compatibility of Community law with national law fall to be determined by the Court.

While the dominant principle is that municipal law will arise as a matter of fact for the CCJ, it has to be clearly understood that questions of Community law will be questions of law, not questions of fact, for the courts of Member States, and the latter must take judicial notice thereof. This fundamental issue has to be explicitly articulated in legislation emplacing the Court, as in the case of the United Kingdom's European Communities Act, 1972 (the "EC Act").[150] This means, further, that it will be practically impossible for municipal courts to avoid decisions of the regional tribunal, even where their State is not a party to a dispute. Hence, the precedent value of judgments will widen beyond the apparently narrow scope of the provision.

VI. *Locus Standi for Natural and Legal Persons*

Although recent trends in International Criminal Law and Humanitarian Law are radically altering the role of natural persons before international tribunals, it is reasonable to say that, with respect to trade and economic interactions, it is still usual for the State of nationality to espouse claims of aggrieved individuals. The European Community moved away from this radically when, in the Treaty of Rome, it gave natural and legal persons *locus standi*.[151] This right has flourished from the narrowest of beginnings where national or Community actions "directly affected" or were "directly applicable" to these persons.[152] The new regime in CARICOM could not ignore the fact that economic integration and the Single Market and Economy were not about abstract factors of production, but were intended to benefit persons. The dispute settlement regime had to be cognizant of these developments and so Article 222 of the Revised Treaty establishes the grounds on which these persons may approach the Court, as parties, by way of special leave.[153]

First, the Court will decide whether "in any particular case this Treaty intended that a right or benefit be conferred by or under this Treaty on a Contracting Party shall enure to the benefit of such persons directly."[154] The

---

150. See European Communities Act, 1972, c. 68 (UK) [hereinafter EC Act].

151. See EEC Treaty, *supra* note 78, art. 173.

152. For a thorough discussion of the case law on this question, see Arnull, *supra* note 137, at 106-43.

153. See Revised Treaty, *supra* note 2, art. 222.

154. Id.

individual then has to establish that he or she has been "prejudiced in respect of the enjoyment of the right or benefit." Further, the individual must establish that the Contracting Party entitled to espouse the claim has "omitted or declined" to do so or, conversely, has "expressly agreed that the persons concerned may espouse the claim instead of the Contracting Party so entitled."[155]

Where this ostensibly cumulative threshold has been met and "the Court has found that the interest of justice requires that the persons be allowed to espouse the claim" then it will so order.[156] It is the view of the present author that if the CCJ approaches the task of interpreting and applying the Revised Treaty on the basis of the purposive and teleological mode of treaty interpretation, it will seek to ascertain whether a right or benefit did in fact exist and was prejudiced, and, thereafter, it will ask itself whether the interest of justice calls for its intervention.

These are evidentiary issues, and the fact is that dilatory behavior on the part of the State entitled to espouse the claim may make it even worse for the potential litigant. It will be observed that the steps are conjunctive. The view could be posited that this will not pose an insuperable bar to those entities gaining access to the CCJ if the latter follows its older "peers" – international tribunals – and approach the interpretation and application of the Revised Treaty from the "objects and purpose" perspective. The importance attached to fundamental rights by the ECJ has already been noted. This approach has already been matched at the municipal level by the ruling of the Judicial Committee in *Gairy v. Attorney-General of Grenada*,[157] where it was held that:

> It is in no way inconsistent for an independent State, while continuing to bear full allegiance to the Crown, to circumscribe the historic rights, powers and immunities pertaining to the Crown in its governmental capacity . . . . Historic common law doctrines restricting the liability of the Crown or its amenability to suit could not stand in the way of effective protection of fundamental rights guaranteed by the [State's] Constitution.[158]

This ruling already forms precedent for those Member States of the Community for which the Judicial Committee is the tribunal of final instance. It is submitted that counsel making this plea within the context of the Court's

---

155. Id.
156. Id.
157. *Gairy v. Attorney General of Grenada*, [2002] 1 App. Cas. 178 (P.C. 2001).
158. Id.

original jurisdiction may very well find traction. Here, again, one would find a situation where the nature of the issue being litigated creates cross-current, in terms of affecting both legal systems in the Community.

There is obviously a very important linkage between individual access to an international tribunal and the terms in which that tribunal expresses displeasure at a Member State's infringement of international obligation, which infringement materially (including financially) affects natural and legal persons. The European Court of Justice has already blazed the trail whereby members of the EU can now be held financially liable for breaches of the Treaty.[159]

A. The Referral Procedure

The foregoing notwithstanding, the view is still firmly held that the referral procedure will provide the greatest scope for individual natural or legal persons to access that tribunal. As far as this procedure is concerned, CARICOM has modified the approach taken by the Treaty of Rome. Under Article 177, now Article 234, of the Consolidated Version of the Treaty Establishing the European Community, the ECJ is empowered to give preliminary rulings on the interpretation of the Treaty and the validity of acts of the institutions.[160] Discretion is given to tribunals in arriving at a decision on whether an approach should be made to the ECJ: "[w]here ...a question is raised before any court or tribunal of a Member State, that court or tribunal may, if it considers it necessary to enable it to give judgment, request the Court of Justice to give a ruling thereon."[161] However, at final instances within the Member States, the discretion is removed: "Where any such question is raised in a case pending before a court or tribunal of as Member State against which there is no judicial

---

159. See Klaus-Dieter Borchardt, The ABC of Community Law 88-93 (2000) (discussing *Brasserie du Pecheur v. Bundesrepublik Deutshcland* and *The Queen v. Secretary of State for Transport ex parte Factortame Ltd.,* Joined Cases C-46/93 & C-48/93, [1996] E.C.R. I-1029, [1996] 1 C.M.L.R. 889).

160. Consolidated version of the Treaty establishing the European Community, art. 234, O.J. C 325/33, at 273-74 (2002), 37 I.L.M. 79, 126 [hereinafter Consolidated EC Treaty], incorporating changes made by Treaty of Nice amending the Treaty on European Union, the Treaties establishing the European Communities and certain related acts, Feb. 26, 2001, O.J. C 80/1 (2001) [hereinafter Treaty of Nice] (amending Treaty on European Union ("TEU"), Treaty establishing the European Community ("EC Treaty"), Treaty establishing the European Coal and Steel Community ("ECSC Treaty"), and Treaty establishing the European Atomic Energy Community ("Euratom Treaty") and renumbering articles of TEU and EC Treaty).

161. Id.

remedy under national law, that court or tribunal shall bring the matter before the Court of Justice."[162]

One hopes that CARICOM will not have to go through the contortions that the English judiciary put itself and the country through, before a clear and precise legal duty is agreed upon. Article 214 of the Revised Treaty provides:

> Where a national court or tribunal of a Member State is seised of an issue whose resolution involves a question concerning the interpretation or application of the Treaty, the court or tribunal concerned shall, if it considers that a decision on the question is necessary to enable it to deliver judgment, refer the question to the Court for determination before delivering judgment.[163]

It is to be noted that a case involving whether a tribunal erred in referring (or not referring) can begin at the lowest level municipally and end up at the final instance (Caribbean Court of Justice – appellate jurisdiction) and then be referred by that national court or tribunal to the judicial organ of the Community (Caribbean Court of Justice – original jurisdiction) for the question to be answered. The international court will not deal with the merits of the issue; that is for the municipal court. Thus, it is quite conceivable that, for those countries that temporarily retain the JCPC as their final instance court, the latter could send a question to the CCJ for answering, if the matter traversed from first instance all the way up. The Judicial Committee would then remit the matter to a lower level tribunal, or itself apply the answers from the regional court to the fact of the dispute at hand. On the other hand, one is quite certain that the Judicial Committee would decline jurisdiction were it invited to intervene (seize itself of jurisdiction) in an issue which clearly involved the interpretation and application of the Revised Treaty. To do any less would be to invite a diplomatic firestorm between the United Kingdom and the Caribbean Community, as opposed to an individual Member State thereof. In fact, the U.K. would be susceptible to State Responsibility being attached.

With that in mind, it is apposite to quickly examine some elements of the case law around the similar procedure in the ECJ. This has important exoteric implications in the development of the necessary "body of Community Law."

It is necessary first to clearly and precisely establish whether the body referring is a "court" or a "tribunal" in the judicial sense of the terms. In

---

162. Id.
163. Revised Treaty, *supra* note 2, art. 214.

Dorsch Consult,[164] the ECJ stated that the following criteria must be taken into account in such a determination:

(a) whether the body is established by law;

(b) whether it is permanent;

(c) whether its jurisdiction is compulsory;

(d) whether its procedure is adversarial;

(e) whether it applies rules of law; and

(f) whether it is independent.[165]

In the joined cases *Gabalfrisa SL and Others and Agencia Estatal de Aministracion Tributaria (AEAT)*,[166] the ECJ had to deal with the issue of whether the referring body was independent. It concerned an economic and administrative tribunal in Spain, the Tribunale Economico Administrativa. This entity has jurisdiction to hear and decide final complaints with respect to a kind of internal administrative action. The Court found that: "a separation of functions was ensured by the law between, on the one hand, the departments of tax and authority and, on the other, the Tribunal…which ruled on complaints without receiving any instructions from the authority."[167] Hence, the referring body "had the character of a third party in relation to the departments which adopted the decision forming the subject matter of the complaint and the independence necessary for them to be regarded as courts or tribunals for the purposes of the Treaty…."[168]

New ground was broken in 1999 in the case *DeHaan Beheer v. Inspecteur der Invoerrechten en Accijuzen te Rotterdam*,[169] where on a preliminary ruling the Court declared invalid a decision of the Commission which had not been directly involved in the instant case. The Court applied what was termed the "principle of procedural economy," in that the question of the legal validity of the Community act had been raised directly in another case which stayed pending judgment in *De Haan Beheer*. Similarly, of legal importance is the approach taken when questions are posed improperly. The Order of the Court in *Rouhollah Nour v. Burgen landische Gebiets Krankenkasse*[170] deals with this extensively.

---

164. *Dorsch Consult Ingenieurgesellschaft mbH v. Bundesbaugesellschaft Berlin mbH*, Case C-54/96, [1997] E.C.R. I-4961, [1998] 2 C.M.L.R. 237.

165. Id.

166. Joined Cases C-110/98 & C-147/98, O.J. C 149/6 (2000).

167. Id.

168. Id.

169. Case 61/98, [1999] E.C.R. 1-5003.

170. Case 361/97, [1998] E.C.R. 1-3101.

B. The Contemporary Application of the Preliminary Ruling Procedure by the European Court of Justice [171]

Where a national court is required to apply provisions of Community Law in a case before it, it may stay the proceedings and ask the Court of Justice for clarification as to the validity of the Community instrument and/or an interpretation of the instrument. The Court of Justice may respond in the form of a judgment instead of an advisory opinion; this highlights the mandatory nature of the preliminary ruling procedure, which is not a contentious procedure but rather one stage of a case that begins and ends in national courts. The object of the preliminary ruling is to secure a uniform interpretation of Community Law and, with it, the unity of the legal order. Alongside this latter function, the procedure is also important to protecting individual rights. The national courts can only assess the compatibility of national and Community law and, in the event of any incompatibility, enforce Community law – which takes precedence and is directly applicable – if the content and scope of Community provisions are clearly set out. This clarity can only be brought about by a preliminary ruling, which means that proceedings for such a ruling offer Community citizens an opportunity to challenge actions of their own Member State that contravene provisions of Community law and ensure enforcement of the latter before national courts.

To a certain degree, the fact that preliminary ruling proceedings serve a dual function compensates for restricting individuals from directly filing actions before the Court of Justice. It is thus crucial for the legal protection of the individual.

In terms of the subject matter, the ECJ rules on the interpretation of instruments and examines the validity of acts of the institutions. Provisions of national law cannot be the subject of a preliminary ruling, yet this fact is often neglected in the questions referred to the Court. Although procedurally inadmissible, the Court of Justice does not simply refer these questions back to the national court; instead, it reinterprets the question as a request by the referring court for basic or essential criteria for interpreting the Community legal provisions concerned, thus enabling it to then give its own assessment of compatibility between national and Community law. The process by which this is done involves extracting from the documentation submitted – particularly the grounds for referral – those elements of Community law which need to be interpreted for the purpose of the underlying legal dispute.

---

171. Passages of this section were first voiced in my Article 'Signposts', *supra* note 73.

The capacity to proceed extends to "all the courts of the Member States." This phrase should be understood within the meaning of Community law. Moreover, it focuses not on the name, but rather the function and position of the judicial body within the systems of legal protection in the Member States. On this basis "courts" are understood to mean all independent institutions that are empowered to settle disputes in a constitutional State under due process of law. By virtue of this definition, the constitutional courts in the Member States and dispute-settling authorities outside the State judicial systems – but not private arbitration tribunals – are also entitled to refer cases.

The overriding criterion in the national court's decision of whether or not to refer will be the relevance of the point of Community law at issue for the settlement of the dispute before it. Naturally, this is a matter for the referring court to assess. The parties can only request, not require, the national court to refer a case. The ECJ considers the relevance of the point in terms of whether the question concerned is amenable to referral; whether a genuine legal dispute is involved; or whether a merely hypothetical issue is being raised, or whether it relates to a point of law that has already been settled. The Court exercises great restraint in applying these criteria and declining requests. However, the system is being reformed and greater stringency is being urged. Of particular note is the insistence that the referral contain sufficiently clear and detailed information on the factual and legal background to the original proceedings. Where this is not provided, the Court declares itself unable to give a proper interpretation of Community law and on that basis rejects the application for a preliminary ruling as inadmissible. The provisions cited previously also demonstrate that there is a level of obligation to refer. A national court from whose decision there is no judicial remedy in law is obliged to refer the issue of Community law pleaded.

The concept of appeal encompasses all forms of legal redress by which a court ruling may be reviewed in fact and in law (appeal) or only in law (appeal on points of law). The concept does not encompass ordinary legal remedies with limited and specific effects (for example, new proceedings, constitutional complaints). Again as will be seen, a court obliged to refer may only avoid doing so if the question is of no material importance for the outcome of the case before it, or has already been answered by the Court of Justice, or the interpretation of Community law is not open to reasonable doubt.

However, the obligation to refer is unconditional where the validity of a Community instrument is at issue. The Court's attitude in this respect has always been that it alone has the power to reject, as illegal, provisions of

Community law. The national court must therefore apply and comply with Community law until it is declared invalid by the Court of Justice. A special arrangement applies to courts in proceedings for the granting of provisional legal protection. According to recent judgments of the Court of Justice, national courts are empowered, subject to certain conditions, to suspend enforcement of a national administrative act deriving from a Community regulation, or to issue interim orders in order to provisionally determine the arrangements of legal relations while disregarding an existing provision of Community law. Failure to discharge the obligation to refer constitutes an infringement of the Treaty, possibly making the Member State concerned liable to infringement proceedings. In practice, the effects of such a course of action have been limited given that the government concerned cannot comply with any order issued by the European Court of Justice because the independence of its judiciary and the principle of separation of powers mean that it is unable to give instructions to national courts. On the other hand, concomitant with the recognition of the principle of Member States' liability to comply is, the possibility of individuals filing for damages which may have arisen from the State's failure to meet the duly contracted obligation to refer. This offers better prospects of success.

In terms of the effects of the preliminary ruling (issued in the form of a court order), it is directly binding on the referring court and all other courts hearing the same case. Even more importantly, in practice it also has a very high status as a precedent for subsequent cases of a similar nature.

The role and value of this procedure elicits declarations such as the following by the Commission of the European Communities:

> The preliminary ruling procedure is undoubtedly the keystone of the Community's legal order. Forty years' experience have shown that it is the most effective means of securing the uniform application of Community law throughout the Union and that it is an exceptional factor for integration owing to the simple, direct dialogue which it establishes with national courts.[172]

Given the current stage in the process to inaugurate and operationalize the CCJ a pre-emptive discussion may be useful. Certain issues surrounding the judicial system of the EU have been the focus of analysis for years and were the subject of consideration by an Inter-Governmental conference. A Working Party was established by the Commission in May 1999 and adopted its report

---

172. European Commission, 'Additional Commission contribution to the Intergovernmental Conference on Institutional Reform: Reform of the Community Courts 2000', at 3 (2000), available at http://europa.eu.int/comm/archives/igc2000/offdoc/cont04022000_en.pdf

(the "WP Report") in January of 2000.[173] One of the startling features noted was that preliminary rulings increased from 141 in 1990 to 246 in 1998, an 87% increase.[174] If that were to happen in CARICOM, there could be a crisis of no mean proportions. Therefore, it may be prudent to assess the findings of the Working Party to ascertain what we may begin to think about when similar problems arise in our own arrangements. The ensuing discussion therefore draws heavily on those findings, repeating some directly, making an effort to adapt others, or plainly presenting them and offering relevant comments thereon.

The WP Report rejected a suggestion that involved "making courts of final instance the only courts entitled to refer questions."[175] For similar reasons it rejected another proposal to exclude only references from national courts of first instance.[176]

It has already been indicated that CARICOM did not opt for any of these extremes. All first instance courts are included, while at the same time enabling superior courts to make referrals automatically incorporates final instance courts. Additionally, the fact that "other tribunals" could make referrals means that some first instance bodies will be able to engage in dialogue with the CCJ. In the case of the Working Party, the decision to reject the proposals arose from the fact that up to the end of 1998, some three-quarters of the preliminary questions referred, came from first instance courts: "[T]herefore...to deny access to the Court...for the national courts which have hitherto referred the great majority of preliminary questions would make excessive inroads into the co-operation and dialogue which must be maintained between national courts and Community Courts."[177] The Working Party took the view that this kind of reform could have a perverse effect at the national level.[178] This would occur by way of litigants being encouraged "or at least the richer ones, to pursue their cases right through to the very highest courts in order to gain access to the Court of Justice by referring a question for a preliminary ruling."[179]

---

173. See Working Party for the European Commission, 'Report by the Working Party on the Future of the European Communities' Court System 2000' (2000) available at http://europa.eu.int/comm/dgs/legal_service/docs/due_en.pdf [hereinafter WP Report].

174. See id. at 3.

175. Id. at 12.

176. Id. at 13.

177. Id.

178. Id.

179. WP Report, *supra* note 173, at 13.

On the other hand, in the words of the report, the "aim is definitely not to create congestion in national courts of final instance."[180]

The idea was also floated that national courts be left to settle all questions of Community law by themselves, with the parties only entitlement being to bring the national judgment "in a sort of longstop appeal claiming breach of Community law."[181] A rejection of this approach was posited on the basis that national courts should be able to deal with issues of Community law in the exercise of their national jurisdiction by being "entitled or obliged" to refer questions to the supreme judicial body, and this without having to pass through a hierarchy of national courts.[182] In their own words to accept such as proposal would be to: "debase the entire system of cooperation established by the Treaties...a system that has proved its worth."[183]

The analysis turned instead to other ways of reforming the system and concomitantly reducing the caseload of the ECJ. First of all, national courts should be encouraged to be bolder in applying Community law themselves. This involved three dimensions (actually proposed in the report as Treaty amendments):

- the first consists in stating the fundamental principle that the courts of Member States have full authority to deal with questions of Community law which they encounter, subject only to their right or their duty to refer questions to the Court for preliminary rulings.[184]

- the second consists of informing courts other than those of final instance (for whom the only option is to refer), that they must try not to refer questions systematically. When assessing the advisability of referring a question such courts "should consider both the importance of the question in terms of Community law and whether there is reasonable doubt about the answer. In other words they should be dissuaded from referring matters to the Court...where Community law clearly states what the answer should be or where the point raised has no legal significance."[185]

The WP Report points out that the notion of reasonable doubt was already clarified in *Cilfit v. Ministry of Health*[186] and that it would be for the ECJ to

---

180. Id.
181. Id.
182. Id.
183. Id.
184. Id. at 14.
185. Id. at 14-15.
186. See Case 283/81, [1982] E.C.R. 3415, [1983] 1 C.M.L.R. 472.

determine whether there needs to be greater flexibility in its application.[187] In terms of the notion of significance for Community law, this fits in with the maxim *de minimis non curat preator*.[188] Here again, it was for the Court, when asked by national tribunals, to state the precise scope that should be given to this notion.[189] It is appropriate to stress here that the attitude towards both the *acte claire* and the significance notions doctrines will be of some importance as the Caribbean Court begins grappling with these problems.

The third dimension relevant to this discussion is stated by the Working Party as follows: "the obligation is imposed on courts of final instance to consult the Court…when a question of Community law is raised before them. In practice, it has not always been possible to follow such a rigid obligation."[190] With that in mind, the Working Party expressed the belief that there should be an obligation imposed upon courts of final instance to refer only questions which are "sufficiently important for Community law" and about whose resolution there remains "reasonable doubt" after having been examined by lower courts.[191]

From the CARICOM perspective, this lack of rigidity already exists in that while there is a duty to refer, the Court still has to answer the question whether "it considers that a decision on the question is necessary to enable it to deliver judgment."[192] If the court makes a decision which the litigants believe is the incorrect one, they have the option of having a higher court make the reference to the CCJ or seeking, to have that institution review the decision under the direct contentious procedure provided for in Article 211. In fact, the Working Party went on to stress that this approach would not pose a threat to the uniform application of Community law.[193] There would still be two ways of remedying any breach by a court of final instance, at least where such a breach resulted in a decision which conflicted with Community law:

- the first is for any other court in the same or another Member State to consult the Court…on the point of Community law in question;

187. See WP Report, *supra* note 173, at 15.
188. See id.
189. See id.
190. Id.
191. Id.
192. See Revised Treaty, *supra* note 2, art. 214 (stating that "the court or tribunal concerned shall, if it considers that a decision on the question is necessary to enable it to deliver judgment, refer the question to the Court for determination before delivering judgment") (emphasis added).
193. See WP Report, *supra* note 173, at 16.

- the second is for the Commission to bring an action for failure to fulfill its obligations against the Member State whose court has shown ignorance of Community law.[194]

These remedies would also be available in the Caribbean Community context.

The WP Report also stressed that in the final analysis, the Commission, as guardian of the Treaties, could ask the Court to decide the question, without setting any time limit.[195] The resulting decisions would restore the uniform application of Community law for the future.[196]

A fourth dimension emerges as well: This is the requirement that a national court must consult the Court of Justice when it proposes not to apply a Community act on the grounds of invalidity. The Group took the view that this should be incorporated in the Treaty. While we are still some time away from that stage, it is arguable that through recourse to the CCJ by the community organ or institution concerned, a Member State or natural or legal persons with *locus standi* could operate to cure this defect.

In terms of irrelevant, premature, or poorly-prepared references, and those which concern only the specific application of Community law and not its interpretation, the Working Party proposed that "mandatory provisions, failure to comply with which would render references inadmissible should be incorporated in the rules of Procedure."[197] These could be supplemented with recommendations from the Court, including possibly a standard model for the formulation of references.

This proposal appears suitable for the CCJ, as it would assist in the institution setting out on the correct footing. Two other suggestions eminently suited to the Caribbean context involve provisions being placed in the Rules of Procedure:

i)   the option of the regional judicial body replying at any stage in the procedure, to the national court, by means of reasoned order where the reply is obvious. An example where this approach would be applicable includes where there can be no reasonable doubt as to interpretation.[198]

ii)   Secondly, encouraging national courts, but not obliging them, to include in the preliminary questions reasoned grounds for the answers

---

194. Id.
195. Id.
196. Id.
197. WP Report, *supra* note 173, at 17.
198. Id.

that those courts consider most appropriate. Where the regional court concurs, it would reply specifying its reasoning by reference to the reasons given by the national court.[199]

The report was quite anxious that the essential purpose of the proposals was to allow national courts to be better placed to give informed decisions on the growing number of Community law issues facing them. On the other hand, only the most resolute action on the part of Member States could secure this objective. The action envisaged by the Working Party is of "direct applicability" to the Caribbean Community in the thrust to establish its own Court of Justice.[200]

Two focal points for action by Member States were identified:

> [F]irst, there is an urgent need to give better training in Community law to all those involved in referring questions for preliminary rulings, be they judges or lawyers. The training should be complete and not just – as is too often the case at the moment – confined to a description of the Community institutions, without a detailed study of the case law.[201]

While there is as yet no "case law" in a judicial sense, in respect to CARICOM, the fact is that the regional universities and the Organs of the Community, together with the Private and Public Bar and the Judiciary, should be engaged in seminars, symposia, and short and long courses on the CSME and the implications for its establishment with a judicial body to oversee compliance with its rules. The case law of other regional integration movements could then be applied, as appropriate, to assess possible courses of judicial action in respect to specific rights and obligations.

Moreover, "powerful information systems should be made available to practitioners, providing them with easy access to the latest information on Community legislation and case law."[202] In line with the actions envisaged, the WP Report recommended that,

> the Member States set up national information centres on Community law, with computer links to the Commission's departments and to the Court of Justices's Research and Documentation Service. Run by experienced specialists in Community law, these would give invaluable aid to national judges and lawyers to enable them gradually to settle, under proper conditions, an increasing number of

---

199. Id.
200. See id.
201. Id. at 19.
202. Id.

difficulties themselves, which for lack of adequate information they currently refer to the Court of Justice.[203]

While the Project Co-Ordinating Unit for the Establishment of the CCJ has made certain proposals to the Regional Judicial and Legal Services Commission research and documentation issues, the truth is that this linkage to the national dimension is not articulated therein. Adoption of this idea, generalized across the two facets of the CCJ's jurisdiction would make a signal contribution to the enhancement of the justice systems in the Member States of CARICOM.

The foregoing represented the reformist proposals advanced. There were more radical suggestions as well. They are being reproduced here to ensure the completeness of the discussion. Three such proposals were advanced, two of which could be seen as relevant to the current context. These are that "the Member States might set up devolved judicial bodies specializing in preliminary rulings; and the Court might select certain questions from among those referred to it."[204] The setting up of the devolved courts at the national level was seen as having the advantages of relieving the ECJ of examining those preliminary questions that were not specially important for the purposes of Community law, as well as reducing administrative costs and time lags – both major problems in our regional justice systems.[205]

On the other hand, there were serious disadvantages. In the first instance, the preliminary ruling procedure involves a dialogue between the referring court, which is hearing the principal action and which alone is fully familiar with the case, and the Community court, which alone is capable of securing a uniform interpretation of Community law. It was felt that to interpose another court between these two would jeopardize the objective of uniform application of the law, "even if the new court were obliged to refer specially significant question to the Court of Justice."[206] There would now be three courts considering the same issues in succession, thereby prolonging the proceedings. The view was also taken that the outcome would be essentially the same even if the questions were first submitted to the regional court for assessment, with the less important ones being remitted to the devolved court.[207] In the latter scenario, a degree of uniformity could be assured, but the advantages of devolution would be mostly lost in the process.[208] Another critical disadvantage

---

203. WP Report, *supra* note 173, at 19.
204. Id. at 20.
205. Id.
206. Id.
207. Id. at 21.
208. Id.

of this route is the fact that the administration of devolved courts would entail heavy outlays in financial, human and material resources, which are not available, and also it could distort the national court structure.[209]

The other "radical" proposal involved giving the ECJ itself the ability to select those preliminary questions that it felt were sufficiently significant for the purposes of Community law.[210] Other questions would be sent back to the referring court "possibly with observations that could help national judiciaries," a procedure similar to that which obtains in the practice of the U.S. Supreme Court.[211] The report took the view that, while this would be simple, effective, and economical,

> such an arrangement cannot be transposed at present to a system of courts which is radically different from the United States: unlike the American system, the Community courts and national courts are not ranked in a hierarchical relationship to each other – the system is based entirely on cooperation and dialogue . . . . It is this cooperation and dialogue which would be upset by such a crude form of selection as that just described.[212]

This "crude" proposal in the EU context is of direct relevance in terms of the Caribbean Court of Justice's relationship to national courts, as there is indeed a hierarchical relationship based on the Article 221 requirement regarding precedent and *stare decisis*. Ultimately it will be up to the President of the Court, his colleagues on the bench and the RJLSC to work out some model that can avoid some of the problems the European system faced forty years after its establishment. One thing is certain, the problems will come, here, much more quickly. In consequence, there may be a future need for a less offensive selection process. This would not go as far as devolution, but would give greater responsibility on national courts to carefully select reference questions. Additionally, it provides a filtration mechanism which may be usefully adopted after the new institution has "cut its teeth" into its tasks, but before the envisaged "flood" of references.

C. Advisory Opinions

1. Caribbean Court of Justice

Treaty Article 212 grants the Court advisory opinion jurisdiction: "The court shall have exclusive jurisdiction to deliver advisory opinions concerning the

209. WP Report, *supra* note 173, at 21.
210. Id.
211. Id.
212. Id.

interpretation or application of the Treaty."[213]   The CARICOM judicial
authority can deliver said opinions "only at the request of the Contracting
Parties or the Community."[214] This will indeed provide a very powerful tool
by which the Organs and Institutions of the Community can promote the
growth and development of its legal order, even if Member States are reluctant
to use this procedure. In addition, there is already something of a clamor for
the category of entities to which this procedure is available to be widened to
include natural and legal persons. The rationale for the latter proposal is that
within the Member States, Constitutional Courts can and are requested to
give opinions on important issues by way of references. The Draft Rules
(Original Jurisdiction) deal extensively with this procedure.

One may compare the CCJ's advisory opinion jurisdiction with two other
tribunals: first, the European Free Trade Area Court of Justice (the "EFTA
Court"). Given that this institution is less well known than the other tribunals
discussed, it is appropriate to provide a brief background. The EFTA Court
was established by the Members of that regional economic grouping who are
parties to the European Economic Area ("EEA") Agreement of 1992 and which
entered into force in 1994.[215] The EFTA was established in 1960 by the
Stockholm Convention, three years after the Treaty of Rome constituting the
European Communities entered into force.[216] The Agreement itself was
between the then twelve members of the European Communities and the
EFTA States Austria, Finland, Iceland, Liechtenstein, Norway, Sweden and
Switzerland.[217] Since that time Austria, Finland and Sweden joined the
European Union on January 1, 1995. Switzerland and Leichtenstein did not
join the EEA Agreement, but the latter acceded on January 1, 1995.[218]

The EFTA Court originally had five Judges, but is now comprised of three
appointed by the Governments of Iceland, Leichtenstein and Norway. The
key instruments constituting this tribunal, which are important for present
purposes, are the EEA Agreement[219] and the Agreement between the EFTA
States on the Establishment of a Surveillance Authority and a Court of Justice

---

213. See Revised Treaty, *supra* note 2, art. 212.

214. Id.

215. See 'What is EFTA?', State Secretariat for Economic Affairs, at http://www.seco-admin.ch/
      themen/aussenwirtschaft/efta/was/?lang=en (last visited Feb. 12, 2004)

216. See id.

217. See id.

218. See id.

219. EFTA Secretariat, The European Economic Area (EEA) Agreement at http://secretariat.efta.int/
      Web/EuropeanEconomicArea/EEAAgreement/EEAAgreement (last visited Feb. 12, 2004)
      [hereinafter EEA Agreement].

("ESA/CJ Agreement").[220] Article 108(2) of the former requires that the EFTA States shall establish a Court of Justice (the EFTA Court).[221] It continues:

> The EFTA Court shall, in accordance with a separate agreement between the EFTA States, with regard to the application of this Agreement be competent, in particular, for:
> (a) actions concerning the surveillance procedure regarding EFTA States;
> (b) appeals concerning decisions in the field of competition taken by the EFTA Surveillance Authority;
> (c) the settlement of disputes between two or more EFTA States.[222]

Protocol 34 to this instrument allows EFTA States the facility of making references to the ECJ where the EEA Agreement rules are identical to those of the European Communities.[223]

The ESA/CJ Agreement highlights Article 108(2) in its Preamble and then goes on:

> RECALLING the objectives of the Contracting Parties to the EEA Agreement, in full deference to the independence of the courts, to arrive and maintain a uniform interpretation and application of the EEA Agreement and those provisions of the Community legislation which are substantially reproduced in that Agreement and to arrive at an equal treatment of individuals and economic operators as regards the four freedoms and the conditions of competition.[224]

After all, when the idea of this accord emerged in 1984, it was envisaged as creating a European Economic Space. Part IV of the ESA/CJ Agreement deals with the judicial institution. Article 27 establishes the Court and adds that it "shall function in accordance with the provisions of this Agreement and of the EEA Agreement."[225] Article 32 confers jurisdiction, which shall be in actions "concerning the settlement of disputes between two or more EFTA States regarding the interpretation or application of the EEA Agreement, the Agreement on a Standing Committee of the EFTA States or the present Agreement."[226] Article 34 is the advisory jurisdiction provision: "The EFTA

---

220. The Agreement between the EFTA States on the Establishment of a Surveillance Authority and a Court of Justice, O.J. L 344 (Dec. 31, 1994) [hereinafter EFTA Surveillance and Court Agreement].
221. EEA Agreement, *supra* note 219, art. 108(2).
222. Id.
223. See id.
224. EFTA Surveillance and Court Agreement, *supra* note 220, at pmbl.
225. Id. art. 27.
226. Id. art. 32.

Court shall have jurisdiction to give advisory opinions on the interpretation of the EEA Agreement."[227] The ECJ model is followed in that "[w]here such a question is raised before any court or tribunal in an EFTA State, that court or tribunal may, if it considers it necessary to enable it to give judgment, request the EFTA Court to give such an opinion."[228]

In juxtaposition to the EU context, it is necessary to modify the application of this procedure in respect of the EFTA States, for reasons including the absence of supra-nationality in the regime. In consequence, the third paragraph of this Article gives the State some discretion to limit the procedure: "An EFTA State may in its internal legislation limit the right to request such an advisory opinion to courts and tribunals against whose decisions there is no judicial remedy under national law."[229] In other words, the Member State may consider it desirable to extend to all its courts the authority to make the request, or it may curtail that authority to the level of last instance courts and tribunals. The determining factors here would include the domestic judicial hierarchy as well as other constitutional law features. Also, unlike in the EU and CARICOM, EFTA is also an entity that enjoys the right to request an opinion from the ECJ – an external tribunal.

In terms of the European Court of Justice, however, the advisory opinion jurisdiction has been placed in the context of the external relations of the Communities: Article 300(6) of the Consolidated Version stipulates that:

> The European Parliament, the Council, the Commission or a Member State may obtain the opinion of the Court of Justice as to whether an agreement envisaged is compatible with the provisions of this Treaty. Where the opinion of Justice is adverse, the agreement may enter into force only in accordance with Article 48 of the Treaty on European Union.[230]

The cited article authorizes the Commission or a Member State to propose amendments to the constituent instruments of the Union. However, it also sets up a process of consultation and the convening of an Inter-Governmental Conference. The Court is placed as the final arbiter in terms of the respective areas of treaty-making competence of the institutions of the Community and individual Member States. This is borne out by Article 107(2) of the Rules of

---

227. Id. art. 34.
228. Id.
229. Id.
230. Consolidated EC Treaty, *supra* note 160, art. 300(6), O.J. C 325/33, at 151 (2002), 37 I.L.M. at 139 (ex Article 228).

Procedure of the ECJ. It states: "The Opinion may deal not only with the question of whether the envisaged agreement is compatible with the provisions of the EC Treaty but also with the question whether the Community or any Community institution has the power to enter into that agreement."[231]

On the other hand, the Member States can be impugned under other provisions for breach of their obligations if they conclude treaties deemed incompatible with the laws of the Community. It may therefore be concluded that the EFTA model uses the advisory opinion procedure to achieve the same effect as the preliminary ruling procedure of the EU. The Caribbean Community has opted to employ both, but it has reserved the former procedure for use by the Community and Member States. Nothing prevents the CCJ from being asked to pronounce on the treaty-making power of the Community under the Revised Treaty. Therefore, the advisory procedure in CARICOM may be used for the purposes sought to be achieved in the EU, as the following demonstrates.

The Conference is empowered under Article 12 (3) to conclude treaties: "Save as otherwise provided in this Treaty, the Conference shall be the final authority for the conclusion of treaties on behalf of the Community and for entering into relationships between the Community and international organizations and States."

The Community has concluded a large number of treaties, and there are also intra-Community Inter-Governmental Agreements.[232] In addition, the Conference may also "consult with entities within the Caribbean Region or with other organizations and for this purposes may establish such machinery as it considers necessary."[233]

While this grant of authority is clear, it is possible for future litigation to arise on the issue of whether a bilateral arrangement concluded by a Member State or a group of such States (for example, the OECS) directly or indirectly impacts upon the Community and therefore arguably falls within the above competence.

Similarly, following the proposed text of some articles in the Free Trade Area of the America's Draft Agreement, it will be possible for Member States

---

231. Rules of Procedure of the Court of Justice of the European Communities, art. 107(2) (1991).
232. The Community has concluded Free Trade Agreements with Colombia, Costa Rica, Cuba, The Dominican Republic, and Venezuela. It negotiates with the European Union as a group, within the African, Caribbean and Pacific Group of States [ACP] established under the Georgetown Accord at the time of the First Lome Convention.
233. Revised Treaty, *supra* note 2, art. 12, para. 9.

to enter into arrangements which impact upon fundamental objectives of the Community. In that situation, it could be argued to be an infringement of the Conference's power. If this were to occur, the CCJ may be minded to adopt the approach of the European Court in the *ERTA* case.[234] The Court held that

> To determine in a particular case the Community's authority to enter into international agreements, regard must be had to the whole scheme of the Treaty no less than to its substantive provisions.

> Such authority arises not only from an express conferment by the Treaty...but may equally flow from other provisions of the Treaty and from measures adopted, within the framework of those provisions, by the Community institutions.

> In particular, each time the Community, with a view to implementing a common policy envisaged by the Treaty, adopts provisions laying down common rules...the Member States no longer have the right, acting individually or even collectively, to undertake obligations with third countries which affect those rules.

> As and when such common rules come into being, the Community alone is in a position to assume and carry out contractual obligations towards third countries affecting the whole sphere of application of the Community legal system.[235]

Then the following key conclusion was drawn: "With regard to the implementation of the provisions of the Treaty the system of internal Community measures may not therefore be separated from external relations."[236] All commentators agree that this case and a subsequent line of similar decisions expanded the range of implied powers of the EC, objectively necessary in order to avoid a disjunct between the fundamental internal objectives and external imperatives required to put the latter into effect.[237]

As discussed above, the Revised Treaty empowers the Supreme Organ to negotiate and conclude international agreements on behalf of the Community. A Member State could request of the CCJ, by way of the advisory opinion jurisdiction, to expatiate on the limits of that competence, vis-à-vis its own sovereign authority in the issue.[238] On the other hand, the rules in Article

---

234. See *Commission v. Council*, Case 22/70, [1971] E.C.R. 263 (1971); see also Arnull, *supra* note 137, at 540-42.

235. *Commission v. Council*, at grounds 15-18.

236. Id. at summary 1.

237. See, for example, Arnull, *supra* note 137, at 540-42.

238. In fact, there was recent disagreement between two Member States with respect to a soon-to-be-concluded FTA with a third State.

80, which proved so difficult to negotiate and which circumscribes the treaty-making competence of members in their bilateral relations with third States, groups of States, or other entities, can form the basis of litigation. Organs of the Community or other Member States can allege breaches of those provisions and request advisory opinions from the Court.

2.　The Appellate Jurisdiction

A critical manifestation of the *sui generis* nature of the CCJ is the fact that Part III of the Agreement covering this jurisdiction is not mentioned in the Revised Treaty. The Commonwealth Caribbean Member States (founders of the Community) have taken and reiterated decisions dating back to 1987 to establish a final court of appeal in substitution for the Judicial Committee of the Privy Council. However, to the extent that in this emanation the Court will be a municipal court of last resort, as I have argued, there is some scope for disagreement with a thesis that the CCJ is the judicial arm of the movement.

Professor Simeon McIntosh disagrees strongly with this "bifurcation." Speaking on the topic of legal education and the CCJ he says:

> I understand [the topic] to mean that we are asked to engage in a critical rethinking of legal education in the region in light of the coming into being of the CCJ to replace the Privy Council, and also to exercise original jurisdiction . . . . I should therefore wish to locate my discussion in a broader conceptual context of an ideal conception of legal education in the region that would best prepare our citizens for the practice of law before the Court, for the practice of law as judges and as academics, and for the practice of law as legislators and policy makers . . . .[239]

But why this "broader conception"?

> This sort of contextualizing, I believe, would help us overcome an emerging perception of a bifurcated court – a court of original jurisdiction requiring *specialist* judges to adjudicate matters pertaining to the operation of the CSME and the interpretation of the Treaty; and a court of appellate jurisdiction to address all cases in law and equity coming from the [M]ember [S]tates' courts of appeal, and requiring different skills from those relevant to the to the original jurisdiction . . . .[240]

This Caribbean jurist prefers a holistic conception of the CCJ in the following terms:

---

239. Simeon C.R. McIntosh, 'Legal Education and the CCJ', based on a presentation at a Symposium on the CCJ in St. George's, Grenada (Sept. 23, 2003), at 2 (on file with author).
240. Id. at 2-3 (emphasis in original).

It is therefore submitted that the authoritativeness of the Court would derive from the fact that it is to be the court of final jurisdiction for the region. There are however matters of such moment that we would not wish to entrust to the state courts, in the first instance, given that we run the risk that [S]tate courts may be too inclined to interpret the Treaty in a manner favorable to the interests of their respective [S]tates. Also it might be too long a process before we have a final and binding decision on appeal from the [S]tate courts to the CCJ. Assigning original jurisdiction to the CCJ…therefore serves the critical values of certainty, efficiency and stability – values that are indispensable for the successful operation of a market economy such as the CSME.[241]

The correct approach is therefore taken with the setting out of all the provisions relating to the municipal court in the Agreement.

The CCJ Agreement recites the main constitutional provisions of the Commonwealth Caribbean Members of the Community, which all send final appeals to the Privy Council. The only exception is Guyana, which terminated appeals to that body in 1966 and which now has to add a third appellate tier. This is already provided for in the Constitution of that Member State. The CCJ Agreement also allows for Member States to enter a reservation to the appellate jurisdiction with the consent of the Contracting Parties.[242]

No reservation is allowed in respect of the original jurisdiction under the CCJ Agreement. However, by virtue of Article 237 of the Revised Treaty, reservations may be entered to Treaty provisions with the consent of the signatory States.[243] It is submitted that a reservation in respect of judicial settlement of disputes would be unacceptable, as it would be incompatible with one of the fundamental objectives of the Treaty, as required under the Vienna Convention on the Law of Treaties.

Article XXV, paragraph 1 of the CCJ Agreement provides that in the exercise of its appellate jurisdiction, "the Court is a superior Court of record with such jurisdiction and powers as are conferred on it by this Agreement or by the Constitution or any law of a Contracting Party."[244] The distinct heads of appeal are set out in paragraphs 2, 3, and 4:

> 2.   Appeals shall lie to the Court from decisions of the Court of Appeal of a Contracting Party as of right in the following cases:
>> (a)   final decisions in civil proceedings where the matter in dispute on appeal to the Court is of the value of not less than twenty-five

---

241. Id. at 3-4.

242. See CCJ Agreement, *supra* note 103, art. XXXIX.

243. See Revised Treaty, *supra* note 2, art. 237.

244. See CCJ Agreement, *supra* note 103, art. XXV, para. 1.

thousand dollars Eastern Caribbean currency (EC$25,000) or where the appeal involves directly or indirectly a claim or a question respecting property or a right of the aforesaid value;

(b) final decisions in proceedings for dissolution or nullity of marriage;

(c) final decisions in any civil or other proceedings which involve a question as to the interpretation of the Constitution of the Contracting Party;

(d) final decisions given in the exercise of the jurisdiction conferred upon a superior court of a Contracting Party relating to redress for contravention of the provisions of the Constitution of a Contracting Party for the protection of fundamental rights;

(e) final decisions given in the exercise of the jurisdiction conferred on a superior court of a Contracting Party relating to the determination of any question for which a right of access to the superior court of a Contracting Party is expressly provided by its Constitution;

(f) such other cases as may be prescribed by any law of the Contracting Party.

3. An appeal shall lie to the Court with the leave of the Court of Appeal of a Contracting Party from the decisions of the Court of Appeal in the following cases:

(a) final decisions in any civil proceedings where, in the opinion of the Court of Appeal, the question involved in the appeal is one that by reason of its great general or public importance or otherwise, ought to be submitted to the Court;

(b) Such other cases as may be prescribed by any law of the Contracting Party.

4. Subject to paragraph 2, an appeal shall lie to the Court with the special leave of the Court from any decision of the Court of Appeal of a Contracting Party in any civil or criminal matter.[245]

Consistent with the approach taken at the time of independence in relation to matters such as citizenship and elections to Parliament, paragraph 5 bars appeal on stipulated matters:

Nothing in this Article shall apply to matters in relation to which the decision of the Court of Appeal of a Contracting Party is, at the time of the entry into force of the Agreement pursuant to the Constitution or any other law of that Party, declared to be final.[246]

---

245. Id.
246. Id.

The Judicial Committee was, by virtue of this provision in the applicable national Constitutions, barred from seizing itself of jurisdiction over these matters. It is to be noted that this form of constitutional bar has been proposed as a possible approach for those Member States that have referenda or other challenging constitutional requirement in emplacing the appellate jurisdiction, but who along with all the others have to give domestic legal effect to the original jurisdiction. The possibility of the CCJ, as the final appellate court of a Member State, being required to refer matters to the Court as an international tribunal has already been discussed.

3. Institutional Distinctiveness

As regards the modalities utilized for appointing the Judges and naming the President, it is incontrovertible that the Caribbean Court of Justice is the only international judicial tribunal with an independent mechanism for carrying out these functions. While the bench of all other international tribunals are appointed by member governments either directly or via elections, the CCJ Agreement establishes in Article V a Regional Judicial and Legal Services Commission.[247] Furthermore, in order to reinforce the Court's insulation from the political executive, there are no Government representatives on the Commission. Its membership is as follows:

(a) the President who shall be the Chairman of the Commission;

(b) two persons nominated jointly by the Organization of Commonwealth Caribbean Bar Association (OCCBA) and the Organization of Eastern Caribbean States (OECS) Bar Association;

(c) one chairman of the Judicial Services Commission of a Contracting Party selected in rotation in the English alphabetical order for a period of three years;

(d) one chairman of a Public Services Commission of a Contracting Party selected in rotation in the reverse English alphabetical order for a period of three years;

(e) two persons from civil society nominated jointly by the Secretary-General of the Community and the Director-General of the OECS for a period of three years following consultations with regional non-governmental organizations;

(f) two distinguished jurist nominated jointly by the Dean of Faculty of Law of the University of the West Indies, the Deans of Faculties of Law

---

247. Id. art. V.

of any of the Contracting Parties, together with the Chairman of the Council of Legal Education; and

(g) two persons nominated jointly by the Bar or Law Associations of the Contracting Parties.[248]

Given that the President will chair the Commission, the Agreement allows for the appointment of a "first-time" Commission. Under Article VI, this is constituted "under the hand of the Heads of Judiciaries of the Contracting Parties."[249] The Commission has been inaugurated and is busy carrying out its tasks.[250] The tasks entrusted to this entity are set out in Article V, paragraph 3, they include:

(a) making appointments to the office of Judge of the Court, other than that of President;

(b) making appointment of those officials and employees referred to in Article XXVII and for determining salaries and allowances to be paid to such officials and employees;

(c) the determination of the terms and conditions of services of officials and employees; and

(d) the termination of appointments in accordance with the provisions of this Agreement.[251]

Paragraph 3 also empowers the Commission to exercise disciplinary control over the Judges, other than the President, as well as over officials of the Court.[252] The disciplinary procedure involves the constitution of a tribunal comprised of senior judicial officers of the Contracting Parties. The tribunal hears the matter and makes recommendations to the Commission. Article IV, paragraph 7 sets out the procedure for appointing or removing the Judges. A majority vote of the Commission is required.[253] With respect to the President, he shall be: "appointed or removed by the qualified majority vote of three quarters of the Contracting Parties on the recommendation of the Commission."[254] Given the infamy of the unit veto in the Community, the Agreement avoided requiring

---

248. Id.

249. Id. art. VI, para. 2(b).

250. It should be noted that the *travaux préparatoires* of the negotiations leading up to the signature of the Agreement will disclose that the various collegia set out were encouraged to take note of the fact of membership of two countries with civil law systems.

251. CCJ Agreement, *supra* note 103, art. V, para. 3(1).

252. Id. art. V, para. 3(2).

253. See id. art. IV, para. 7.

254. See id. art. IV, para. 6.

unanimity, but set a high threshold. Accordingly, any Head of Government of a Contracting Party who opposes a nomination by the Commission has to secure the concurrence of three-quarters of his or her peers. Additionally, the Heads of the Contracting Parties are precluded from substituting their candidate, if they negative a recommendation from the Commission. They have to remit the matter to that body for another recommendation. The President is appointed by letter under the hand of the Chairman of the Conference, while the Judges are appointed by letter under the hand of the Chairman of the Commission, that is, the President.

In terms of the sources from which the bench of the Court can be drawn, Article IV, paragraph 10 mandates that the candidate

> is or has been for a period or periods amounting in the aggregate to not less than five years, a Judge of a court of unlimited jurisdiction in civil and criminal matters in the territory of a Contracting Party or in some part of the Commonwealth, or in a State exercising civil law jurisprudence common to Contracting Parties, or a court having jurisdiction in appeals from any such court and who, in the opinion of the Commission has distinguished himself or herself in that office.[255]

The Agreement does not exclude non-judicial jurists, and sub-paragraph (b) grants eligibility to persons engaged in the practice or teaching of law for periods of no less than fifteen years in the aggregate.[256] The other stipulations set out above are applicable.

It should be noted that even while speaking of developing an "indigenous jurisprudence," allowance is made for members of the bench to be drawn from outside of the Member States. The possibility for candidates from civil law jurisdictions is self-evident: Haiti and Suriname are full Members of the Community. But in addition, it is not the feeling of those who crafted the regime that the jurisprudence being sought to be created necessarily involves any extreme notion of self-reliance – a sort of legal autarchy. There are many examples of jurists coming into the region from outside and making valuable contributions. The difference with the Privy Council experience is that their Lordships are writing law for societies they have great difficulty in empathizing with in terms of cultural mores, socio-economic and political values, and so on. This was recently openly admitted by a Senior Law Lord, The Right Honorable Lord Leonard Hoffman:

---

255. Id. art. IV, para. 10.
256. Id.

It is an extraordinary fact that for nearly nine years I have been a member of the final court of appeal for the independent Republic of Trinidad and Tobago, a confident democracy with its own culture and national values, and this is the first time that I have set foot upon the islands. No one unaware of the historic links between the islands and the United Kingdom would believe it possible.[257]

He then makes the following observation:

Although the Privy Council has done its best to serve the Caribbean and, I venture to think, has done much to improve the administration of justice…our remoteness from the community has been a handicap. We have been necessarily cautious in doing anything which might be seen as inappropriate in local conditions and although this caution may have occasionally saved us from doing the wrong thing, I am sure it has also sometimes inhibited us from doing the right thing.[258]

Of equal importance in terms of the need to acquire juristic talent from outside the region, is the requirement in Article IV paragraph 1 that: "the Judges of the Court shall be the President and not more than nine other Judges of whom at least three shall possess expertise in international law including international trade law."[259] The fact is that, at the present time, neither as products of the system of legal education, nor within the ranks of those engaged in the practice of law, could there be said to exist a "surfeit" of international legal expertise. The Council for Legal Education, spurred on by efforts of the Project Co-Ordinating Unit, has recently tabled proposals to the Legal Affairs Committee which should see to the closing of this "deficit."

Another indisputable first for the CCJ is the mode of financing the Court. In order to allay fears that the institution may be manipulated by the political executive through its financing, or that its sustainability may be compromised, the Conference of Heads of Government accepted a recommendation that a trust fund be established. Hence, the Caribbean Court of Justice Trust Fund (the "Trust Fund") was constituted by The Agreement Establishing the Caribbean Court of Justice Trust Fund. Within that legally binding international instrument, the Contracting Parties agree to the levels of financial contribution they will make.

Technical studies were done leading to a finding that with an investment of US$100 million, the Court could be financed sustainably, in perpetuity and thus secure its complete independence. The Caribbean Development

---

257. The Right Hon. Lord Leonard Hoffman, Speech at the Annual Dinner of the Law Association of Trinidad and Tobago, at 5 (October 10, 2003) (transcript on file with author).

258. Id. The Association is, even at this stage of the process, on the record as opposing the establishment of the Court.

259. CCJ Agreement, *supra* note 103, art. IV, para. 1.

Bank ("CDB") was mandated to raise that amount on the international capital markets. The Contracting Parties have agreed loans with the CDB in the amount of their contribution to the budget of the Court.

Yet another unique feature of the regime is the composition of the Board of Trustees. Again, there are no governmental representatives. Instead a number of pan-Caribbean entities were invited to make nominations. All happily concurred. They are:

- the Secretary-General of the Community;
- the Vice-Chancellor of the University of the West Indies;
- the President of the Insurance Association of the Caribbean;
- the Chairman of the Association of Indigenous Banks of the Caribbean;
- the President of the Caribbean Instituted of Chartered Accountants;
- the President of the Organization of Commonwealth Caribbean Bar Associations;
- the Chairman of the Conference of Heads of Judiciaries of the Member States of the Caribbean Community;
- the President of the Caribbean Association of Industry and Commerce; and
- the President of the Caribbean Congress of Labour.

In structuring the Board of Trustees in this manner, greater public confidence in the entire regime is engendered, as there can be no thought of governments manipulating these persons. In fact several other regional bodies have requested to serve on the Board.

One issue which has driven the affected members of the Caribbean Community to begin the move away from the Privy Council is the question of access to justice. The fact is only a small number of persons can access the JCPC. The large corporations that can afford it naturally wish the Committee to be retained. In criminal cases, matters in *forma pauperis* form the bulk of litigation, particularly death penalty cases. With that in mind, from the earliest discussion of a regional court, it has been agreed that while the CCJ would have a permanent seat in Port-of-Spain, the capital of Trinidad and Tobago, it would operate as an itinerant, peripatetic tribunal, like the former Federal Supreme Court and the extant OECS Supreme Court. This is provided for in the CCJ Agreement, Article III, paragraph 3, which stipulates that the Seat of the Court will be in the territory of a Contracting Party as agreed by a qualified majority thereof, "but, as circumstances warrant, the Court may sit in the territory of any other Contracting Party."[260]

Finally, as regards compliance and specifically enforcement of judgments, the CCJ Agreement requires the parties to take all the steps necessary to have enforcement done on the same basis as the decisions of their superior courts, and to have all their authorities act in aid of the Court.[261]

The distinctiveness of the Court would be further enhanced if the Member States were minded to adopt proposals emanating from the Expert Group of Heads of Government.   On the nexus between implementation and enforceability they propose:

> As regards enforceability, the [West Indian Commission] envisaged that the CARICOM Supreme Court (now the Caribbean Court of Justice…) would have the competence to issue an Order of Implementation in appropriate cases involving the upholding of rights and duties under Community law. We believe this to be the right conceptual approach.[262]

In fact, if this approach is conjoined with the adoption by Member States of legislation similar in concept to the U.K.'s European Communities Act, 1972,[263] then the issue of supranationality is avoided while the objective being sought is attained. The Expert Group of Heads of Government favours this approach:

> In its Report, the West Indian Commission had set out how [a system of enforcement] could work through draft Instruments of Implementation and appropriate national legislation. The system would lead to the development of a coherent body of Community law. It is a system under which the [Executive] Commission would prepare a Draft Instrument…to give effect to (or, sometimes to facilitate the making of) a Community Decision. That "draft" Instrument of Implementation [then] would be formally approved (with or without modification) by Heads of Government or other competent body.[264]

The Instrument would be "declaratory of rights and duties arising under the Decision," but it would not "itself have statutory effect."[265] This gap would be closed by a revision of the Revised Treaty, in which

---

260. Id. art. III, para. 3.
261. See id. art. XXVI.
262. Regional Integration, *supra* note 4, at 4.
263. EC Act, *supra* note 150.
264. Regional Integration, *supra* note 4, at 4.
265. Id.

Governments would undertake to enact national legislation (perhaps through a basic 'CARICOM Act' in each member country) which would give legal effect in that country to the rights and duties arising under [all] Instruments of Implementation. This would be the way in which a body of Community law would be developed consistent with CARICOM remaining a Community of Sovereign States. . . .[266]

The European Union, in the drive to transform itself from a Community into the Union, utilized the modality of the Single European Act, 1986.[267] This was a treaty, but its provisions were to be ratified *en bloc* by the Member States. The Caribbean Community may not wish to adopt that approach, but rather have an identical piece of draft legislation for its Member States to enact. With that in mind, we may examine the provisions of the EC Act, in which the U.K. enacted the supranationality of the European Community into its municipal domain.[268]

As is known, in the U.K., the majority of international legal obligations contracted by the Crown have to be incorporated into municipal law before they can bind the citizens. (In rare cases, some treaties may produce self-executing effects, and rules of customary international law whether in a treaty or not, are binding *erga omnes*.) The Interpretative provision of the EC Act lists EC instruments affected by the legislation and defines "treaty" to include "any international agreement, and any protocol or annex to a treaty or international agreement."[269] Section 2, entitled "General Implementation of Treaties," is the main operative provision. It prescribes as follows:

(1) All such rights, powers, liabilities, obligations and restrictions from time to time created or arising by or under the Treaties, and all such remedies and procedures from time to time provided for by or under the Treaties, as in accordance with the Treaties are without further enactment to be given legal effect or used in the United Kingdom shall be recognized and available in law, and be enforced, allowed and followed accordingly; and the expression "enforceable Community right" and similar expressions shall be read as referring to one to which this subsection applies.[270]

The U.K. was thus able to retain Parliamentary Sovereignty while faithfully adhering to the obligations it had contracted into, upon accession into the

---

266. Id.
267. Single European Act 1986, O.J. L 169/1 (1987), [1987] 2 C.M.L.R. 741 [hereinafter SEA] (amending Treaty establishing European Economic Community, Mar. 25, 1957, 298 U.N.T.S. 11).
268. EC Act, *supra* note 150.
269. See id. s. 1(4).
270. Id. s. 2(1).

supranational Community. The spirit of the Governance proposals being advanced in the Caribbean Community clearly requires that the Member States be prepared to adopt a similar approach. The "enforceable Community rights" are of obvious significance for natural and legal persons as it is these rights in the Revised Treaty constituting the CSME that will form the subject matters in actions before municipal courts – to which the referral procedure would apply – and in instances where natural or legal persons apply for special leave to have the CCJ determine their grievances.

In the EU, the Court of Justice has, from the outset, been very determined that Member States comply with their obligations. Thus in an early, precedent-setting judgment *Commission v. Italy*, it affirmed:

> In permitting Member states to profit from the advantages of the Community, the Treaty imposes upon them also the obligation to respect its rules.

> For a State unilaterally to break, according to its own conception of national interest, the equilibrium between advantages and obligations flowing from its adherence to the Community brings into question the equality of Member States before Community law and creates discrimination at the expense of their nationals, and above all of the nationals of the State which places itself outside the Community rules.[271]

As Professor Arnull observes, following the judgment, "it is no defense that national legislation, although technically incompatible with Community law, is in practice applied in accordance with the requirements of the Treaty."[272] This in fact "gives rise to an ambiguous state of affairs by maintaining, as regards those subject to the law who are concerned, a state of uncertainty as to the possibilities available to them of relying on Community law."[273]

Subsection 2 of Section 2 of the EC Act goes on to provide the procedural route by which future rights and obligations can pass into the municipal domain without the need for primary legislation. Thus, a Regulation, Order-in-Council, or an act of a designated Minister or Department may make provisions:

(a) for the purpose of implementing any Community obligation of the United Kingdom, or enabling any such obligation to be implemented, or of enabling any rights enjoyed or to be enjoyed by the United Kingdom under or by virtue of the Treaties to be exercised; or

---

271. *Commission v. Italy*, Case 39/72 [1973] E.C.R. 101; see Arnull, *supra* note 137, at 26-27.
272. Arnull, *supra* note 137, at 26-27.
273. Id.

    (b) for the purpose of dealing with matters arising out of or related to any such obligation or rights or the coming into force, or the operation from time to time, of subsection (1) above.[274]

Careful note is to be taken of the subtle draftsmanship. The "rights enjoyed or to be enjoyed" inure to the benefit of the United Kingdom, and then through it, to natural and legal persons.[275] There is also a very interesting rider which qualifies the two provisions, by empowering or giving discretion to the persons exercising the statutory authority granted: That person "may have regard to the objects of the Communities and to any such obligations or rights as aforesaid."[276] Of course it is the case, and it has often happened, that where the discretion is not exercised or is exercised improperly in relation to Community law, either the Commission of the Communities or the Court of Justice has intervened to correct the situation.

    It is also important to cite, in part, Section 3 entitled "Decisions on, and proof of, Treaties and Community Instruments etc.":

> (1) For the purposes of all legal proceedings any question as to the meaning or effect of any of the Treaties, or as to the validity, meaning or effect of any Community instrument, shall be treated as a question of law (and, if not referred to the European Court, be for determination as such in accordance with the principles laid down by and any relevant decision of the European Court).[277]

The section goes on to require that judicial notice be taken of the Official Journal of the Communities, as well as of "any decision of, or expression of opinion by, the European Court" on any question mentioned in the previous provision.[278] This provision accords substantively with the discussion above on the issue of the legal quality of Community law within the municipal domain, as opposed to municipal law in matters before the regional court.

    It is submitted that the Caribbean Community could imaginatively adapt this piece of legislation to craft its own "Single CARICOM Act," and therein include by reference, or directly, provisions relating to the jurisdiction of the CCJ, in relation to Orders of Implementation.

---

274. EC Act, *supra* note 150, s. 2(2).
275. Id.
276. Id. s. 2(2).
277. Id. s. 3(1).
278. Id. s. 3(2).

CONCLUSION

The Caribbean Community is at a very critical stage of its development. After being in existence for thirty years, and being the oldest regional integration regime among developing countries, it has accepted the challenge to reach a higher level of engagement involving the rule-based approach. This approach permeates the Revised Treaty. As with the results of the Uruguay Round of Multilateral Trade Negotiations, attempts were made to ensure legal symmetry in the entire regime, including the Dispute Settlement provisions. The Caribbean Court of Justice sits at the top of the dispute settlement "totem pole." This institution, in addition to having the responsibility of interpreting and applying the Revised Treaty, is also the court of final instance for the Commonwealth Caribbean Members of the Community, in place of the Judicial Committee of The Privy Council in London. Uniquely, the cycle of independence is being completed and sovereignty affirmed by these States, while at the same time, in setting up the CCJ as the regional court, they are volitionally ceding aspects of that sovereignty in order to greater facilitate the economic and social development of their people.

The *sui generis* CCJ is quite deserving of accolade for its legal and institutional architecture. The hope is that it will be deserving of even greater accolade as it carries out this challenging task and so truly enhances the law of international organizations.